CHOICES THAT DETERMINE
YOUR DESTINY

THE
JOSEPH
ROAD

JERRY WHITE

NAVPRESS

NavPress is the publishing ministry of The Navigators, an international Christian organization and leader in personal spiritual development. NavPress is committed to helping people grow spiritually and enjoy lives of meaning and hope through personal and group resources that are biblically rooted, culturally relevant, and highly practical.

For a free catalog go to www.NavPress.com or call 1.800.366.7788 in the United States or 1.800.839.4769 in Canada.

© 2009 by Jerry E. White

All rights reserved. No part of this publication may be reproduced in any form without written permission from NavPress, P.O. Box 35001, Colorado Springs, CO 80935. www.navpress.com

NAVPRESS and the NAVPRESS logo are registered trademarks of NavPress. Absence of ® in connection with marks of NavPress or other parties does not indicate an absence of registration of those marks.

ISBN-13: 978-1-60006-269-8

Cover design by DesignWorks Group
Cover image by In-House Art

Some of the anecdotal illustrations in this book are true to life and are included with the permission of the persons involved. All other illustrations are composites of real situations, and any resemblance to people living or dead is coincidental.

Italics in Scripture quotations are the author's emphasis.

Unless otherwise identified, all Scripture quotations in this publication are taken from the *Holy Bible, New International Version®* (NIV®). Copyright © 1973, 1978, 1984 by International Bible Society. Used by permission of Zondervan. All rights reserved. Other versions used include: the New American Standard Bible® (NASB), Copyright © 1960, 1962, 1963, 1968, 1971, 1972, 1973, 1975, 1977, 1995 by The Lockman Foundation. Used by permission; *THE MESSAGE* (MSG). Copyright © 1993, 1994, 1995, 1996, 2000, 2001, 2002. Used by permission of NavPress Publishing Group; *The Living Bible* (TLB), copyright © 1971, used by permission of Tyndale House Publishers, Inc., Wheaton, IL 60189, all rights reserved; and the New King James Version (NKJV). Copyright © 1982 by Thomas Nelson, Inc. Used by permission. All rights reserved.

Library of Congress Cataloging-in-Publication Data

White, Jerry E., 1937-
The Joseph road : choices that determine your destiny / Jerry White.
  p. cm.
Includes bibliographical references (p.   ).
ISBN 978-1-60006-269-8
1. Christian life. 2. Joseph (Son of Jacob) 3. Choice (Psychology)--Religious aspects--Christianity. I. Title.
BV4501.3.W4662 2009
248.4--dc22

                                     2009020814
Printed in the United States of America

1 2 3 4 5 6 7 8 / 13 12 11 10 09

To
The People who have
helped me walk
The Joseph Road

Mary
My lifelong love, friend,
and companion

Dr. Walter Nelson
Who introduced me to Christ

Roger and Joanne Brandt
Dear friends and encouragers
for our entire adult lives

CONTENTS

There is nothing like a dream to create the future. Utopia today, flesh and blood tomorrow.

—Victor Hugo, *Les Misérables*

Joseph had a dream, and when he told it to his brothers, they hated him all the more.

—Genesis 37:5

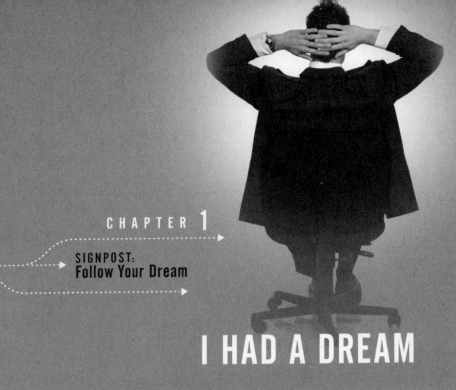

I HAD A DREAM

D o you remember when you dreamed those impossible dreams? To be a baseball star, a model, a fireman, an astronaut, or a pilot? To be rich, to be famous? When did those dreams die?

For most of us, we saw them fade as the reality of life began to set in. This is sad, for dreams can keep us going, give us hope, and propel us to great achievements.

Joseph—this young teen, this privileged son of Jacob—had a dream. A real one, not just some random thought. And in those days, most people put a great deal of credence in dreams.

Afterward, Joseph did what any immature young man would do in the same situation: He told his brothers.

He said to them, "Listen to this dream I had: We were binding sheaves of grain out in the field when suddenly my sheaf rose and stood upright, while your sheaves gathered around mine and bowed down to it."[1]

They interpreted this as signifying their bowing down to their spoiled brat of a brother. This made them mad. They had already "hated him"; now "they hated him all the more."

Then Joseph reported yet another dream. He said he saw "the sun and moon and eleven stars bowing down to me." Joseph told this one to not only his brothers but also his father, Jacob, who rebuked him for such arrogance and insolence. However, "his father kept the matter in mind"; he knew there must be something to it.

We could criticize Joseph's brashness, but maybe he was just being guilelessly honest. He probably was as puzzled over the dreams as his family was. When we're young, we can't easily tell when fantasy ends and truth begins. That's the innocence and imagination of youth.

NEEDING DREAMS

Young and old, we all need dreams. We need a vision that gives us something to work toward. Many of us dreamed of a lovely wife or a handsome husband, about children, about sex sanctified in marriage, about owning a home, about getting a college degree, about having a good job. These dreams and goals kept us going. The vision of a special future keeps us working hard and hoping.

Some of us see God using us in big ways, beyond our wildest

imagination. We rarely tell anyone about these dreams for fear of meeting a response similar to what Joseph received. Yet deep in our inner being, we sense a destiny for our lives.

Do you have a sense of destiny? Or has the burden of life caused you to give up on that?

Each of my daughters has a lovely singing voice. They each use it well. But Kristin really wanted to become a performer, not just in narrow Christian circles but in the wider secular world. This dream of hers seemed so impossible to me. At times, I rained on her parade (as she pointed out). I wanted to believe, but something in my rational, engineering mind doubted.

I well remember a trip we made to Los Angeles. She had tracked down the voice coach who taught such stars as Barbara Streisand. Kristin was able to get an expensive appointment with him for a one-hour lesson.

She did great. He helped her, giving her a tape of her lesson with many valuable insights and suggestions. He also challenged her, emphasizing how difficult it would be to break into the world she envisioned. He told her how hundreds of young men and women with great voices flock into Southern California each year to wait tables and do odd jobs while they train and wait for the big break.

I was scared for her. In my worn-down adulthood, I'd forgotten what it meant to have a dream. I'd forgotten how risky some of my own early undertakings were.

I remember dreaming about the first book I wanted to write. I talked to Dr. Howard Hendricks, gave him an outline and a summary, and waited for his evaluation. He responded, "Go for it—this is great!" I walked away from that conversation totally excited. I began to write, putting reality to the dream.

We all need dreams, and we all need people who encourage those dreams.

DREAMS FROM GOD

In particular, we need God-given dreams.

For Joseph, it became clear in time that God indeed was speaking to him through those unusual dreams in his youth.

Why did God speak that way to him? Joseph could still have prospered without such a dream. Perhaps it simply made him aware that God *does* speak. Perhaps later, when he was in prison, remembering those dreams gave him hope. Knowing that God has spoken and is leading gives us hope in the dark times—and there *will* be dark times for all of us.

Have you ever had God speak to you? Perhaps it wasn't through any audible words, but you just knew God had spoken. We need that. We need to hear from God.

But when is a dream truly from God, and when is it just wild speculation, unfounded in reality? To know the answer, we need to understand how God talks to us. He uses:

- The Scriptures
- His "still small voice"[2]
- Our godly friends
- A Spirit-dominated mind—"Your ears will hear a voice behind you, saying, 'This is the way; walk in it'"[3]

When we hear a word from God, we must listen, understand, and then act.

> If people can't see what God is doing,
>   they stumble all over themselves;
> but when they attend to what he reveals,
>   they are most blessed.[4]

QUESTIONS FOR REFLECTION

1. What were some of your dreams and hopes in your child-hood and teenage years?
2. What events built up those dreams? What events dampened or crushed them?
3. What are your dreams today?
4. How does God fit into those dreams?

Whatever men expect, they soon come to think they have a right to it; the sense of disappointment can, with very little skill on our part, be turned into a sense of injury.
— SENIOR DEVIL SCREWTAPE TO JUNIOR DEVIL WORMWOOD, IN C. S. LEWIS's *THE SCREWTAPE LETTERS*

"Here comes that dreamer!" they said to each other. "Come now, let's kill him and throw him into one of these cisterns and say that a ferocious animal devoured him. Then we'll see what comes of his dreams."
— GENESIS 37:19-20

CHAPTER **2**

SIGNPOST:
Listen to God in the Noise

SHATTERED DREAMS

J oseph's dreams soon brought him a living hell. While his father favored and pampered him, his brothers grew to hate him even more.

Finally they'd had it with Joseph. As he came to them in the fields where they herded their flocks, they hatched an evil plan. "They plotted to kill him."[1] Only his oldest brother, Reuben, kept them from quickly murdering him. "Let's not take his life," Reuben said. "Don't shed any blood." At his suggestion, Joseph was thrown alive into a dried-up cistern. (Reuben had decided to come back later and rescue him.)

From the bottom of this pit, Joseph could hear his brothers laughing, arguing, and plotting. He was helpless. No way out. He pleaded and prayed. He was probably there for hours at least, perhaps even days.

The brothers were still considering killing Joseph, but then a caravan of Midianite traders happened along on their way to Egypt. At this point, brother Judah intervened. "What will we gain if we kill our brother and cover up his blood?" Instead, Judah suggested offering him to the traders as a slave, so the brothers pulled Joseph out of the pit and sold him.

Reuben wasn't on the scene when this transaction occurred, and when he later found out about it, he was devastated. But along with his brothers, he concocted an elaborate scheme to convince their father, Jacob, that Joseph had been killed by a wild animal:

> Then they got Joseph's robe, slaughtered a goat and dipped the robe in the blood. They took the ornamented robe back to their father and said, "We found this. Examine it to see whether it is your son's robe."[2]

Jacob was fully taken in:

> He recognized it and said, "It is my son's robe! Some ferocious animal has devoured him. Joseph has surely been torn to pieces."
>
> Then Jacob tore his clothes, put on sackcloth and mourned for his son many days. All his sons and daughters came to comfort him, but he refused to be comforted. "No," he said, "in mourning will I go down to the grave to my son." So his father wept for him.[3]

For the rest of their lives, these brothers were followed by their guilty consciences over how they'd treated their brother. They never forgot how he responded. Decades later, they would recall, "We saw how distressed he was when he pleaded with us for his life, but we would not listen."[4] They would always remember their frightened teenaged brother pleading for his life. And Reuben would tell them, "Didn't I tell you not to sin against the boy? But you wouldn't listen! Now we must give an accounting for his blood."[5]

TERROR IN A DARK HOLE

Imagine yourself as a young teenager in Joseph's situation: abandoned in a pit, then sold to strangers as a slave. Just think of the terror that must have struck Joseph like a knife in the back.

From his perspective, I imagine the whole thing unfolding like this:

When Joseph first came to his brothers' camp that day, he was immediately grabbed and stripped of the offensive robe—the symbol of their father's favoritism. When they roughed him up and threw him into a dry well, he couldn't believe what was happening to him. He thought at first they were just having some sadistic fun at his expense. Then he overheard their conversation: "Kill him," "teach him a lesson," and much more.

In that dark hole, he began to shake with cold and fear. Surely one of the brothers would come to rescue him. Later he heard a jumble of voices. He could pick up bits and pieces of the trade language. They were negotiating to sell him as a slave! He still couldn't believe this was happening. Fear gripped him even more.

He'd heard of the fate of slaves sold to these Midianite merchants. Even the relief of not being murdered hardly assuaged the reality of the fate of a slave.

Soon a rope came dangling down. He was roughly commanded to put it around his chest and under his armpits. As he was dragged upward, his brothers disappeared. The Midianite traders tied his wrists and shackled his feet. Then the caravan began to move again. He was shoved along roughly.

In his agony, he still imagined at certain moments that his brothers might come and rescue him. But as days and nights ran together, he numbly realized his fate. In his heart, he cried out to God. He wept at night, wondering why God had allowed this.

He wished now he hadn't been so arrogant toward his brothers. In retrospect he could see how he'd provoked their anger and resentment. But it was too late. His fate was sealed, though he had no idea what that fate would be.

The numbness and fear wore off. Survival instincts began to surface. He'd gone from being a privileged son to a piece of property! And his destination was Egypt.

DESPERATE FOR RESCUE

So much for Joseph's dreams.

And so much for God, it would seem.

Have *your* dreams been shattered? Have they faded away because you've been mistreated, misused?

Perhaps you're in the middle of such difficulty right now. You're in a pit crying out, regretting your past, desperate for anyone to rescue you.

Perhaps a divorce is destroying every glimpse of hope you once had for a perfect marriage. Or the drug charge against your son feels as if it's against you personally; you feel you've failed. The latest company downsizing showed you that you weren't valuable enough to keep. Or that word you dreaded to hear—*cancer*—is now part of your reality. That sin you knowingly committed hangs like a lead pipe around your neck. Those words you yelled out in anger have severed a relationship forever.

Whatever the reason—bad choices, alcohol, illness, injury, the cruelty of others—your life has been shattered.

There *is* hope, even though for the present all seems hopeless. There is a way out. There's still a dream to pursue. God still has a plan: *The Joseph Road*, which we'll see spreading out before us in this book.

FIRST, BROKENNESS

The Joseph Road is also the God Plan. You may have set your own course for most of your life, and through hard work, captured opportunities, and timely action, you succeeded. You got the job, the home, the family, the rewards of your labors. You became confident in your own abilities and comfortable in your success.

Then all hell broke loose, and everything began to fall apart. You became disoriented, introspective, disillusioned. You felt abandoned by friends and God.

You admit that God has a plan for you. But the words "In all things God works for the good of those who love him"[6] have a hollow ring. Does God know what He's doing? Is He doing anything at all?

Faith disappears. Your belief system begins to crack. One thing becomes clear to you: Your fate is out of your hands. There's nothing you can do. So you turn to the only option left: You pray. You begin to deal with God at a deeper level than ever before.

Job did that, though at first it seemed fruitless. As the supreme Old Testament example of suffering, stripped of everything he held dear, he said, "I cry out to You for help, but You do not answer me; I stand up, and You turn Your attention against me."[7]

We know Job's story eventually turned out better. But what about *our* stories? We can't see the conclusions to our own stories.

The book of Psalms is full of troubled people crying out to God. It also overflows with God's comfort for them (and for us), as in these words from David:

> The righteous cry out, and *the* LORD *hears* them;
>   *he delivers* them from all their troubles.
> *The* LORD *is close* to the brokenhearted
>   and *saves* those who are crushed in spirit.[8]

Joseph was certainly crushed and brokenhearted after his brothers did their number on him. Perhaps that was the turning point of his life, the moment when he truly surrendered to God. We do know that years later he would look back at what his brothers did to him and say assuredly, "God intended it for good"[9] But when you're still lying there in the pit, such a perspective can seem empty.

In my own life, having passed through the deep waters of burnout as well as the far greater depths of my son's death, I can say only that *it's true*: God *can* make good out of it; God *does* have a plan.

But first comes brokenness.

And when deliverance comes, it's often in the most unexpected ways. Perhaps the only rescue Joseph had any hope for was that his brothers would somehow repent and come tell him, "It's all a joke!" Instead, as we'll see, his "rescue" began with being sold into slavery.

Light shines most brightly
In the midst of darkness.
Hope is nurtured most deeply
In the depths of despair.

QUESTIONS FOR REFLECTION

1. What "pit" are you in now?
2. What are you learning about brokenness?
3. What kind of "rescue" are you looking for?
4. What is your prayer to God at this time?

To walk out of His will is to walk into nowhere.

—C. S. LEWIS, *PERELANDRA*

The LORD was with Joseph and he prospered. . . . The LORD gave him success in everything he did.

—GENESIS 39:2-3

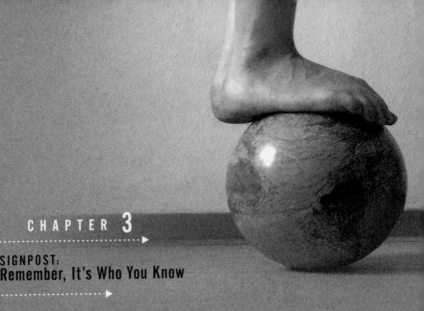

THE SOURCE OF SUCCESS

Have you ever observed a truly gifted or successful person and wondered how they gained such achievement? Was it hard work or sheer luck? Was it through family connections, a wealthy upbringing, or relentless individual effort? Was it achieved with integrity or by ruthlessly using people?

History is filled with examples of each of those scenarios. But there are startling exceptions—lives that defy explanation. These people radiate a special touch on their lives because they know that *God* is the source of their success. It's evident in their spirit. They have nothing of the arrogance of power or the pride of accomplishment. Though others may try to discredit them, they find nothing that sullies their character.

Joseph was a man like that. Reading the entire account of his

25

life clearly demonstrates that he was an intelligent, gifted man. In addition to hearing from God, he was able to navigate the most difficult relationships and events. And he did all this without plotting or manipulating his own success. He was without guile. It's not that he was naïve or lacked ambition; Joseph took advantage of every circumstance and opportunity. But he did it without the scheming and ruthless ambition often seen in the worlds of business and government.

INTO SLAVERY

Joseph's entrance into Egyptian slavery brings to mind the horrible fate of people in centuries past who were torn from their families in Africa and transported to slavery in Europe and America. Nothing in our imagination can conjure up such a terrible experience—the trauma and degradation, the panic, the fears, the smells. No movie comes close to putting us in their shoes.

One of the most striking memories implanted in my mind is from a visit to Ghana, West Africa. I was with a group of African friends as we toured a castle at Cape Coast where slaves were taken before being sold and loaded on ships for Portugal. I walked through the holding cells where hundreds, perhaps thousands, had cowered in terror. I saw the trapdoor in the governor's room through which women were passed for his sexual pleasure.

Seeing all this, I became more and more depressed. As the only Caucasian in our group, I felt a particular discomfort. Then one of my African friends explained to me that the brutality of the white colonizers and slave traders wasn't the only reason for what happened at this castle; African tribesmen had raided neighboring tribes and brought captives there for sale. Those slaves, like Joseph, were victims of their own countrymen. Yet so many of them—also like Joseph—rose up from such injustice to lead lives of incredible impact.

TRANSFORMATION

Here was Joseph—a helpless, pampered teenager, ripped from his family, betrayed by his brothers—now little more than a piece of human flesh.

I imagine his trek to Egypt being something that tested his endurance beyond anything he thought possible. He would have walked while his Midianite captors rode camels. With each step, his worst fears came to pass. There was no escape.

His feet were blistered, but his legs became strong. He was bronzed by the sun. Meanwhile, his captors put him to work whenever the caravan stopped—gathering wood for fires, pitching tents, feeding these enemies, sleeping with the fear that he would be sexually attacked. Survival instincts began to replace the fear. He resolved to not only live but also stay strong. Fortunately he wasn't starved, as he needed to be in reasonable physical condition for sale as a slave when they reached Egypt.

The realization of his fate deepened within him. A hardening of his spirit and body developed as they came closer to Egypt. In the days and weeks, his muscles toughened.

He wondered what his future would be. As the caravan came to the strange land and cities along the Nile, Joseph's arms were bound behind his back and his feet were hobbled to prevent an escape. His captors treated him roughly but without hurting him, so as not to lower the price he would bring.

Arriving at a market square in Egypt's capital city, Joseph was put on display in the slave auction. He'd become a strong, well-built man. The boy had disappeared. But the inner fears and anxieties remained.

Soon Joseph was sold to a wealthy man of high rank—to "Potiphar, an Egyptian who was one of Pharaoh's officials, the captain of the guard,"[1] although Joseph had no idea who Potiphar was.

SUCCESSFUL FOR A REASON

In the account of what happened after Joseph's entry into Potiphar's household, a theme quickly stands out: His life was going in a distinct direction, and there was clearly a reason for it:

The LORD was with Joseph and *he prospered,* and he lived in the house of his Egyptian master. When his master saw that *the LORD was with him* and that *the LORD gave him success in everything he did,* Joseph found favor in his eyes and became his attendant. Potiphar put him in charge of his household, and he entrusted to his care everything he owned.[2]

This summary we're given in Scripture is concise. How did it play out?

As a new slave, Joseph probably began by doing manual labor, cleaning latrines, washing floors, tending animals, and dozens of other undesirable tasks. The way he did these things must have caught Potiphar's eye. Obviously Joseph performed well. He worked hard and didn't complain. He earned Potiphar's trust, leading to Joseph's advancement into more responsibility. He became living evidence of what Jesus later affirmed: "Whoever can be trusted with very little can also be trusted with much."[3]

Now he found himself in a grand house under the watchful eye of the head servant. He didn't know the language but learned quickly to survive. The fears remained, but a resignation to his fate pushed him forward. He simply decided to work hard and be a loyal slave. He decided not to attempt to escape, although the thought crossed his mind almost daily. After all, where would he go and how would he survive?

Joseph had an inner sense of God's presence and prayed much as he'd been taught in his home. But those dreams back in Canaan—now they seemed nonsensical.

By his skill and diligence, he quickly became a household slave rather than a field slave. Potiphar recognized his ability and leadership and gave him increased responsibility.

The length of his service in Potiphar's household was likely between one and three years. Joseph became known, respected, and trusted. He learned the language well. He organized the entire household operation—purchasing, negotiating, and managing its affairs. He became known in the community as Potiphar's head servant.

KEEP GOING

Let's pause Joseph's story for a moment. What are *you* encountering now in your life? Do you feel as though all hell has broken loose? Perhaps it just seems that way, while the reality is simply that life isn't much fun anymore. Worries, fears, pressures, and difficult relationships are wearing you down.

As I've observed my friends, the list of unwanted events in their lives seems endless:

- Financial pressures
- Job loss
- Children on drugs
- Family conflict
- A spouse demanding a divorce
- Failing health
- Untimely deaths

Even when our own list isn't quite so traumatic, we're still barraged by pressures at work, busyness, a hectic schedule. And our shattered dreams get even worse. Like Joseph, we see no way out. So what do we do?

Here's what:

1. We keep going. We don't quit. We draw deeply on our resources in God.
2. We keep doing what we must do. We remain faithful even when we find it hard to be motivated. We take one day at a time.
3. We work and live to the best of our ability with the gifts and skills God has given us. We don't become angry and despondent. And we don't blame others.
4. Then we *wait* for God to act.

And God *will* act—in His own time and way.

BEING WATCHED

There's much we don't know about what Joseph experienced in these days. How long did he work as just an ordinary slave before he was promoted? How was he treated by the "senior" slaves? What went through his mind as he longed for home night after night, asking God to help him?

It's probably a mistake to think that Joseph simply breezed through this time. In his humanity, he undoubtedly had his low moments, his times of anxiety and sleeplessness, as well as further mistreatment from others.

Most important of all, he had no options. As a slave, he had no control of his destiny. He had only his resolve to live well and faithfully before God in his terrible circumstances. And the results of that resolve were clearly seen — and rewarded — by his earthly master. "His master *saw* ... ."[4]; "Joseph found favor *in his eyes*."

When we're going through difficult times, our lives are on display to others. They watch how we respond, especially if we're known to be a follower of Jesus.

Although Joseph worked hard, he knew the God of his forbearer–Abraham, Isaac, and Jacob. Because he knew God, he was blessed beyond his wildest dreams. Knowing God and knowing He has plans for us propels us with a deep resolve. With God as our advocate, who can possibly argue with Him? Similarly, now Jesus Christ gives us an inner power that marks our lives. Joseph was God's instrument for an eternal mission, unknown even to him at the time.

QUESTIONS FOR REFLECTION

1. When you're going through difficult times, how does knowing God help you?
2. What aspect of your life needs your faithfulness and diligence the most right now?
3. Recount some of your successes and disappointments from your past. With each of them, how did you view God at the time and how did you view yourself?

Morality, like art, means drawing a line someplace.

—Oscar Wilde

Joseph was a strikingly handsome man. As time went on, his master's wife became infatuated with Joseph and one day said, "Sleep with me." He wouldn't do it.

—Genesis 39:6-8, msg

CHAPTER **4**

DOING RIGHT, BUT GETTING CRUSHED

Have you ever felt as though you finally "got life together"? You were on top of your game. Your family and job were in balance. You were on your way to seeing long-desired goals grow into reality. Then suddenly—

No, let's not describe it. Let Joseph's dilemma describe it.

As we've seen, Joseph wasn't doing too badly for a slave. He wasn't in some shack behind Potiphar's house; he lived and served in the main home and ran it well. He had every privilege of the owner without being the owner. No doubt he still felt hidden hurts from his past, but he was making the best of a bad situation, and he was successful beyond his wildest expectations.

He was living with purpose and integrity. He was trusted. He was loyal. He was competent.

35

And he was about to get slam-dunked for it.

DAILY TEMPTATION

Potiphar's wife was bored. And when she saw Joseph, "well-built and handsome"[1] and likely much younger, she lusted after him. At first it was innuendos, a slight touch, a look of the eye. But when the slave Joseph didn't respond to her feminine wiles, she gave him a command: "Come to bed with me!"

She demanded this not once but repeatedly—"day after day." She wouldn't give up. She plotted and persisted.

And Joseph repeatedly refused—for good reason—as he carefully explained to her,

With me in charge, my master does not concern himself with anything in the house; everything he owns he has entrusted to my care. No one is greater in this house than I am. My master has withheld nothing from me except you, because you are his wife.[2]

What incredible insight for a young man. And what courage. Was he tempted? You better believe it! Can you imagine the thoughts running through the mind of this virile, handsome young man?

No one would know.

If I don't give in to her, I'll lose my job.

This could really secure my position.

After all I've been through, I deserve a little pleasure.

Moreover, it wasn't at all unusual for wealthy Egyptian masters or their wives to carry on a secret sexual alliance with a servant, safe within their own household.

But Joseph chose to resist.

Why did he refuse to sin? Simple. His view of God kept him from it. God was watching, and Joseph feared God more than he did men. He told Potiphar's wife, "How then could I do such a wicked thing and *sin against God*?"

These aren't just words—platitudes and prudery. Joseph held a deep conviction of who God was and what God expected of him. Even when no one was looking, he knew he couldn't hide from God. He was simply afraid to defy God. Something inside him caused him to fear God more than man. The "who you know" from the previous chapter was God. He feared God more than man.

The pressure from Potiphar's wife grew so intense that "he refused to . . . even be with her," although she daily sought him out.

COLD REALITY

It's likely that Joseph, in his wisdom, also realized that Potiphar would eventually discover any affair between his wife and Joseph. Then what would happen?

With our own temptations, the cold reality of discovery helps to keep overt sin at bay. The fear of being found out checks the natural inclination to indulge in many kinds of sin. Certainly that's true regarding the inner lust and greed battling inside us at all times.

As the events of life impact us unexpectedly, we know we can never go back and rewrite the story. Our fears captivate and control us—as well as condition us. We either give up or toughen up.

Also, like Joseph, we get caught up in events and circumstances we never expected: the loss of a job, a failed marriage,
unjust treatment, financial reversals, and much more. In the midst
of unexpected adversity, our character and our faith encounter
profound testing. Job said, "When he has tested me, I will come
forth as gold."[3] Knowing the result doesn't make it easy. We still
must live through it, both internally and externally.

THE REAL BATTLE

Yet the real battle isn't external but internal: in the mind and in
the heart. That's where fear and anxiety, shame and guilt, pride
and ego struggle to dominate reason and spirit. The battle is one
of hope versus despair, trust versus rebellion, and resolve versus
capitulation. That inner struggle Joseph knew only too well. It
relentlessly tempted him to give up, to quit.

What keeps a man or woman going in such oppressive conditions? Above all else, *hope.* Hope in God's unchanging and unfail-
ing love. Hope in his ultimate sovereignty. Hope in God's ultimate
triumph over evil and injustice. Hope in his *personal* care for us.

Hope goes beyond physical training, intellectual reason, and
even theological knowledge. It springs from a reservoir deep within
that has been conditioned by months and years of saturation in
God's Word and in prayer. It comes from trusting the goodness
of God in the simple areas of life. It comes from the nourishment
that builds the spirit for such times as these.

We'll never know how much of this was known by Joseph
at his young age. Certainly the foundations had been laid by

his father, grandfather, and great-grandfather: Jacob, Isaac, and Abraham. In our own trials, we too have the opportunity to build such a heritage and legacy for our own family.

DOWNFALL

Sin confronts us daily, persistently. But sometimes an encounter with temptation will be life-changing, no matter how we respond. It will test every resolve we have. Giving in will seem so easy — and so pleasurable. And the temptation isn't just sex. It's dishonesty, lack of integrity, greed, anger, slander, hate — all of them bringing us to a point of decision that will drastically impact our lives.

One day, Joseph "went into the house to attend to his duties, and none of the household servants was inside."[4] This woman finally had Joseph alone and unaware. "She caught him by his cloak and said, 'Come to bed with me!' But he left his cloak in her hand and ran out of the house."[5]

Joseph's reaction made her furious. She screamed and yelled — and she took revenge.

To the household servants, she accused Joseph of attempted rape.

> "Look," she said to them, "this Hebrew has been brought to us to make sport of us! He came in here to sleep with me, but I screamed. When he heard me scream for help, he left his cloak beside me and ran out of the house."[6]

She repeated the same lie to Potiphar. He probably saw through his wife's lies; if he'd truly believed her, he most likely would have had Joseph executed without even a trial. A slave's life is cheap.

Whether or not Potiphar believed his wife, he had to do something. So Joseph was thrown into a particular prison "where the king's prisoners were confined."

That was the end of Joseph's upward rise. This man who was so loyal, faithful, and competent had now been destroyed by one huge lie. *Injustice!* Again!

Two lessons emerge in living color:

1. Sin will always confront us, requiring our clear choices in response to those confrontations.
2. Obedience to God's commands can lead to injustice, not success.

For Joseph, it was all so unfair! Yes, and so is much of life. Evil has a way of creating injustice. If you doubt that, look to the plight of the vast majority of people in this world. They're victims of poverty, crime, and injustice, unable to defend themselves.

Where does one turn at times like this, when you do everything you know to do, you remain faithful and still you suffer?

Life crumbles like ashes in your hand.

This is where trust enters the picture. Can we trust God to ultimately bring justice? Can we be assured He'll make the pathways of our life what He wishes? When *The Joseph Road* seems absolutely impossible, will we trust Him? When sin draws us like a moth to a flame, will we turn and run?

We must. And we can. Not on our own strength but in God's. And He will ultimately bless the choices of this path.

But in the heartbreaking reality of your immediate suffering, that's not something you know and can see, is it? Nor did Joseph.

He went to prison. That was his unavoidable next step. And he submitted to what God was doing in his life.

No temptation has seized you except what is common to man. And God is faithful; he will not let you be tempted beyond what you can bear. But when you are tempted, he will also provide a way out so that you can stand up under it.[7]

QUESTIONS FOR REFLECTION

1. How does one resist moral sin?
2. What does it mean to fear God when you're tempted to sin?
3. How should you respond to injustice when it affects you? How should you respond when it affects others?

It is possible that the scrupulously honest man may not grow rich so fast as the unscrupulous and dishonest one; but success will be of a truer kind, earned without fraud or injustice. And even though a man should for a time be unsuccessful, still he must be honest; better to lose all and save character. For character is itself a fortune.

—SAMUEL SMILES

Joseph's master took him and threw him into the jail where the king's prisoners were locked up. But there in jail GOD was still with Joseph: He reached out in kindness to him; he put him on good terms with the head jailer. The head jailer put Joseph in charge of all the prisoners—he ended up managing the whole operation.

—GENESIS 39:20-22, MSG

CHAPTER 5

SIGNPOST:
Keep Getting Up and Doing Good

UP FROM THE ASHES

When Joseph was a child, I'm sure he never tired of hearing his father tell about wrestling with a "man" who proved to be much more than that and about insisting he wouldn't let go until that man blessed him.[1]

Jacob's constant limp was a visual and physical reminder — to himself as well as to his favorite son, Joseph — of that one God. This God, mysterious and powerful, never left Joseph's mind.

He would come to mind when Joseph reflected on the stories of his great-grandfather Abraham and when he puzzled over Abraham's near sacrifice of his son Isaac, Joseph's grandfather.[2] Why would a man even contemplate such an act as to sacrifice his own son? Abraham did it simply because God commanded him to. And God met him there.

COMPLICATIONS

Joseph also would recall the intrigue in his family background. The tension between his uncle and his father, Esau and Jacob, was magnified for these brothers by the favoritism of their father toward one and their mother toward the other.

Then there was Joseph's own position as a father's favored child. He would recall the colorful coat Jacob made him and the memories of his mother, Rachel, whom Jacob also loved best. He would remember the constant tensions among the other three "mothers" and their offspring in Jacob's polygamous family.

Life back then was complicated and now had only become more so. The simplicity of Joseph's youthful dreams were dashed on the roads of reality, although perhaps, in some way, he appreciated being out of that incessant conflict of Jacob's household.

But *this*? Prison? For doing *good*?

Joseph had actually liked Potiphar, who treated him well and had given Joseph his big opportunity. Now Joseph had blown it. Or had he?

Confusion and doubt crowded in as Joseph reviewed every detail of those last days. The screams and hatred of Potiphar's wife replaced the "love" she supposedly expressed for him. Maybe it would have been easier to give in and play the game.

But he could not. The power of the God described by his father constantly arrested him. God seemed distant now yet incredibly close. Joseph sensed a presence he couldn't explain.

NEEDING DELIVERANCE

His dilemma is one we often face at key turning points in our lives.

As a young believer in my teens, I recall near escapes from sin. "Something" just held me back. I remember one of the boys in our youth group flashing a condom from his glove compartment, almost proudly. I was intrigued but repelled.

What about you? When has God delivered you? How is He delivering you now? What is He saying to you in your quiet desperation? Are you listening? The darkness of life can be a place of new discovery.

I remember the darkness that enveloped me after our son's murder. I sat immobilized and numb. Where was God? Why are our lives suddenly impaled with this grief? Up until then, except for a few relatively minor bumps along the road, our lives seemed charmed—four beautiful children, my promotion to brigadier general, becoming president of The Navigators, having books published, receiving respect and honor.

Now this: a son's life taken in a senseless crime.

I was trapped in a cell of despair, puzzled, unable to think clearly. To the best of my knowledge, I had tried to follow God. Mary and I were committed to each other as a couple. We sincerely wanted to be obedient and godly people. *Why this?*

GETTING BACK UP

Like Joseph, I had to wait and gradually rebuild a life that had taken such an inexplicable turn. But unlike Joseph, I wasn't alone. I watched the pain of my daughters and Mary, unable to do anything for them except hold them. There were no adequate words.

The choice was to give up or get up and keep loving God.

When you're knocked down, get up and keep going. That's more than just the American way or a Hollywood cliché or a self-motivation maxim based on fairy tales. To rise up and try again, no matter how many times you fall, involves courage, discipline, and resilience—factors of true greatness in the human realm.

Joseph was a man like that, and more, because his getting back up was the result of his good heart and a deep commitment to his God—the same God his father, Jacob, served.

BUSY DOING GOOD

Even in prison, Joseph began to serve. He did good works. He saw needs and met them. He was competent, even gifted, and he was recognized for his abilities. He was like Jesus, of whom the Scriptures testify, "He has done everything well."[3] It wasn't an "act" on Joseph's part for gaining favor, but the favor did come his way. Soon the prison warden "put Joseph in charge of all those held in the prison, and he was made responsible for all that was done there"[4]

God honored Joseph's commitment and excellence but still kept him in prison.

You may be looking ahead and thinking, *I know this story. When the baker and the cupbearer come on the scene, Joseph will seize his opportunity to get out.* But that was neither Joseph's motive nor his plan. He had no word from God. He saw no future. He simply served and "went around doing good," as Jesus did centuries later.[5] Joseph didn't even try to escape, although perhaps at times he could have done so.

This is the crux of *The Joseph Road*: Not knowing one thing about the future, Joseph simply did good in whatever tasks or opportunities came his way. He had no bargains or promises given him, no "steps to success." He was still a slave—a slave who was now a royal prisoner. Not much to write home about. He was an alien, a captive without possessions, without a promise, without a future.

Perhaps we all reach a point in our lives in which we possess nothing and can do nothing except serve and wait. I imagine that being the case with imprisoned German pastor Dietrich Bonhoeffer. He went about doing good, not giving in to evil, and thereby forfeited his life.

It may also have been the experience of Anne Frank, the Jewish girl who wrote so poignantly from her hiding place, or of Corrie ten Boom, the courageous Dutch woman who suffered for hiding Jews during World War II. Perhaps it was Paul's experience, imprisoned for his faith, and the experience of countless martyrs throughout the centuries whose names are forgotten.

Each one made a difference. They went about doing good even when they could see no end to their desolate circumstances.

Like Joseph, we can't "read ahead" and predict that we'll live happily ever after in this world. Joseph had no idea what the next day would bring. He had to live by God's wisdom—the same wisdom that tells us, "Do not worry about tomorrow"[6] and "Whatever your hand finds to do, do it with all your might."[7]

QUESTIONS FOR REFLECTION

1. What caused Joseph to find favor with the chief jailer?
2. As you reflect on your life or the lives of others, how have you seen that doing good opened doors of opportunity?
3. What helps most to keep a person going when life becomes difficult?

True faithfulness consists of obeying God in all things and in following the light that points out our duty, and the grace which guides us; taking as our rule of life the intention to please God in all things and to do always not only what is acceptable to Him but, if possible, what is most acceptable.

—FRANCOIS FENELON

The LORD was with Joseph and gave him success in whatever he did.

—GENESIS 39:23

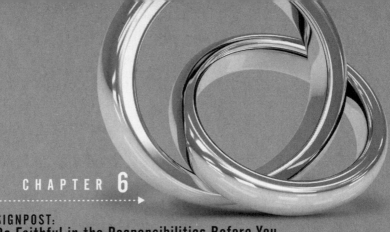

CHAPTER 6

SIGNPOST:
Be Faithful in the Responsibilities Before You

FAITHFULNESS BRINGS FAVOR

For Joseph, what was his life in prison like?

Horrible. No television, no library, no exercise, no weight room. No promise of three meals a day. No expectation of anyone caring or even knowing he was there. We have no record of anyone visiting Joseph, for he had no nearby relatives to provide food or clothing.

He probably had a slab for a bed, a trench for a toilet, and minimal, distasteful food. All were in such stark contrast to the life he'd known in Potiphar's home.

Even after being there for years and having reached the point of being fully trusted by the prison officials, Joseph was still being kept not just in custody but in "the dungeon."[1]

But these hardships are not the focus in the continuing

account of Joseph's story. The Scriptures quickly record that the prison warden came to esteem Joseph and actually put him fully in charge. How could that have happened? The sovereign God whom Joseph trusted was still at work.

A PATTERN IN HIS LIFE

So much had changed for Joseph in going from Potiphar's house to prison, but one huge factor stayed the same: Just as "the LORD was with" Joseph in Potiphar's house and gave him favor in Potiphar's eyes,[2] so also in prison "the LORD was with him" and gave Joseph favor in the warden's eyes.[3]

This God-given favor again raised Joseph into a position of full trust and responsibility. The pattern repeated: Just as Potiphar had placed Joseph "in charge of his household, and he entrusted to his care everything he owned,"[4] so also "the warden put Joseph in charge of all those held in the prison, and he was made responsible for all that was done there."[5]

Once more, Joseph's continued faithfulness brought relief-giving service to the one he recognized as master. Just as Potiphar "did not concern himself with anything except the food he ate" by having Joseph in charge,[6] so also "the warden paid no attention to anything under Joseph's care."[7]

His prominent success still sprang from the same source: Just as in Potiphar's house, where "the LORD gave him success in everything he did,"[8] so it was in prison: "The LORD was with Joseph and gave him success in whatever he did."[9]

WHO IS YOUR GOD?

That's the way the Scriptures concisely summarize Joseph's experiences in prison, bringing out what's most important. In the way it gradually unfolded, I can imagine something like this:

After Joseph was incarcerated, the prison commander would eventually send guards to bring the new prisoner before him. Because the prisoners in this facility were those who had offended royalty and high officials (such as Potiphar), there were always interesting details to learn from them—details that would fuel the fires of gossip about royal rivalries and intrigues.

Furthermore, Joseph was no longer an unknown foreign slave. Potiphar had bragged about this remarkable servant to whom he entrusted ever-greater administrative responsibilities, this Hebrew man with the Midas touch. As Joseph made his regular rounds in the community to purchase food, hire workers, and negotiate the many arrangements necessary to run this significant household, he'd gained a growing reputation. Merchants and bankers knew him. Other royal officials who visited Potiphar would have seen Joseph faithfully attending his duties.

And now, the hottest scandal in ages: Everybody heard about the accusation against Joseph from Potiphar's wife, who had a reputation of her own: a racy one. True or not, believable or not, her charge against Joseph was all anybody talked about.

"So tell me, foreigner," the prison commander would say after his guards brought in the new prisoner. "What really happened?"

"I did nothing."

"Ha! I can well imagine! I've heard the stories about that woman. She wasn't about to let someone as good-looking as you escape her charms. Why didn't you just cooperate? I can assure you, her pleasures are quite real."

"Believe me, I was tempted. But — "

"But what? Didn't you know that her power is as real as her pleasures? Just look where she's got you now!"

"I was more afraid of my God than I was of her."

"Your *God*! You speak as if there is one."

"There is — and only one."

"Ha! Here in Egypt we have many gods, and none of them could care less what you did or didn't do with that woman. Who *is* your God?"

Joseph would then begin explaining the story of his great-grandfather Abraham, his grandfather Isaac, his father, Jacob, and the stories he'd been told from his youth of their encounters with God.

Eventually, however, the commander forced the conversation to a more practical and selfish concern. "I've heard you're an exceptionally hard worker and completely reliable. I want to assign you some tasks."

"I will do as you say."

Bit by bit, Joseph was given more and more work to do. The commander's trust in him kept growing, until finally his responsibility encompassed "all that was done there,"[10] all because (1) the Lord was with Joseph, and (2) the Lord gave him success. Joseph's only responsibility was to do well in what he was assigned.

OUR CALL TO FAITHFUL SERVICE

As followers of Jesus, all of us can know the Lord's presence and protection just as fully as Joseph did. We have this promise from God: "Surely I am with you always."[11]

And just as Joseph was called by God to be faithful in his responsibility, so are we: "Whatever you do, do your work heartily, as for the Lord."[12] Doing that, we'll know God is with us, although it doesn't mean everything will turn out like we wish any more than it did for Joseph.

We can also be assured of "success," as Joseph experienced, though this isn't quite as simple or straightforward as we might like. We aren't promised earthly prosperity. The success we're promised rests totally in God's hands to give when He chooses and in the way He chooses. The Bible is full of stories of God's servants who were faithful yet suffered persecution, hardships, and even martyrdom. History is full of more of the same stories. All through history, there are many who served God wholeheartedly and lost their lives.

In Hebrews 11, we find a list of great successes of faithful men and women. Some accomplished obvious victories and achievements. But that was far from everyone's story:

> Others were tortured. . . . Some faced jeers and flogging, while still others were chained and put in prison. They were stoned; they were sawed in two; they were put to death by the sword. They went about in sheepskins and goatskins, destitute, persecuted and mistreated — the world was not worthy of them. They wandered

in deserts and mountains, and in caves and holes in the ground.[13]

God doesn't owe us anything. He tells us, "In all your ways, acknowledge Him, and He shall direct your paths."[14] But He doesn't say that those paths will be either easy or prosperous.

QUESTIONS FOR REFLECTION

1. Over time, Joseph's life showed prominently the patterns of adverse circumstances, faithfulness on his part, and eventual favor from others and from God. What patterns are most prominent in your life?

2. How real for you, in everyday terms, is the promise that the Lord will always be with you?

3. What responsibilities should you embrace wholeheartedly at this particular season in your life?

We are not to throw away those things which can benefit our neighbour. Goods are called good because they can be used for good: they are instruments for good, in the hands of those who use them properly.

— CLEMENT OF ALEXANDRIA

Remember me and show me kindness.

— GENESIS 40:14

CHAPTER 7

SIGNPOST:
Serve Others

BUILDING OTHER PEOPLE'S DREAMS

A s Joseph the prisoner continued faithfully serving his new master and doing good, two new prisoners joined him. Both had been sent there because they'd angered Pharaoh. Joseph could certainly relate to them, because both had held positions of responsibility and trust: one as Pharaoh's baker; the other as Pharaoh's cupbearer, the steward of his wine. For two such important prisoners, it was Joseph, of course, who was put in charge of them.

Of course, as we have learned from seeing his consistent character so far, Joseph would have been faithful in this responsibility. But he was more than just competent and diligent. The way he served others was not just a matter of duty but of true concern for others. He had that genuineness about him that caused others to open up to him.

A TIME TO CONFIDE

One night, there in prison, both these men had dreams that left them troubled. Joseph, always perceptive and attentive, quickly noticed: "When Joseph came to them the next morning, he saw that they were dejected."[1] He asked them why, and they told him. Apparently Joseph was a man in whom people confided. This was because of his character, not because he wore a badge reading, "Come to me if you have a problem." Doing good leads to insight and involvement with the plight of others, even when our own situation is unclear. I think Joseph had a genuine concern for these prisoners, perhaps because he'd become their friend.

The chief cupbearer was the first to tell Joseph his dream: He had seen a vine with three branches, laden with grapes. "Pharaoh's cup was in my hand, and I took the grapes, squeezed them into Pharaoh's cup and put the cup in his hand."[2]

Joseph quickly interpreted this. "Within three days Pharaoh will lift up your head and restore you to your position, and you will put Pharaoh's cup in his hand, just as you used to do when you were his cupbearer."[3]

Imagine how thrilled the cupbearer must have been to hear this.

Now it was the chief baker's turn. In his dream, he carried three breadbaskets on his head. "In the top basket were all kinds of baked goods for Pharaoh, but the birds were eating them out of the basket on my head."[4]

Joseph's interpretation this time was considerably different: "Within three days Pharaoh will lift off your head and hang you on a tree. And the birds will eat away your flesh."[5]

How did the baker respond to this interpretation? We can easily imagine his fear. At least he would know that Joseph had not tried to hide the truth.

And truth it was. Three days later, on Pharaoh's birthday, he restored the cupbearer to his position, but he hanged the baker—exactly the events that Joseph had foreseen in their dreams.

A WAY OUT?

When Joseph had interpreted the cupbearer's dream, he added a personal request that showed his human desire. "When all goes well with you," he told the cupbearer, "remember me and show me kindness; mention me to Pharaoh and get me out of this prison. For I was forcibly carried off from the land of the Hebrews, and even here I have done nothing to deserve being put in a dungeon."[6]

Were Joseph's motives pure in making this request to the cupbearer? Or was he failing to leave his fate fully in God's hands and instead attempting to manipulate his circumstances? One could argue either way, but Joseph's actions were certainly understandable for a human being who'd been treated so unjustly.

Not that his request mattered. "The chief cupbearer . . . did not remember Joseph; he forgot him."[7] It isn't hard to imagine how that could happen. Perhaps he was so relieved to be back in royal favor and afraid to do anything, however slight, that might raise any questions. Besides, why should he take even a small risk for someone still locked up and out of sight?

Our good deeds often go unrewarded. But we must still keep doing good.

GOD DECIDES

The Joseph Road is littered with roadblocks, glimpses of hope, pleas for mercy, and desires for deliverance from our own problems. *The Joseph Road* isn't a straight road with signs and warnings; it's more like a forest trail that's only faintly marked in places and where we sometimes grope our way along. But it leads in the right direction, to a destination we desire but have never seen.

So what are we to do? We keep serving others and building others' dreams. In God's timing, He'll reward what we've done. When He does, it will be for His honor, not ours.

In four decades of service in the United States Army in the middle of the last century, Lieutenant general William K. Harrison became known as "the Christian general." In those wartime years, he wanted to command an army in the field but never got to do that. He was always in a serving role, faithfully carrying out the orders of his superiors. Finally he was appointed to face the enemy — not in the field, but at the critically important conference table. He was given the lead role in representing the allied forces at the United Nations Armistice Conference to bring an end to the Korean War.

Even when people are ungrateful, we serve them. Even when suffering and injustice comes, we serve. When we have power and succeed, we serve. This is what it means to "love your neighbor as yourself."[8]

Serving others and helping them succeed must be done simply on the basis that it's the right thing to do. We choose to be faithful and do good. Then God decides how He'll bless us.

QUESTIONS FOR REFLECTION

1. In what typical situations in your life is it hardest for you to have a genuine concern for others?
2. How does it affect you when your good deeds go unrewarded?
3. What most convinces you that serving others is the right thing to do?

Those who are readiest to trust God without other evidence than His Word always receive the greatest number of visible evidences of His love.

—Charles G. Trumbull

God has revealed to Pharaoh what he is about to do.

—Genesis 41:25

CHAPTER 8

SIGNPOST:
Expect God to Surprise You — Watch Him Work

A TWIST OF FATE

t seemed like the golden opportunity, and Joseph had certainly seized it. Pharaoh's cupbearer, whom Joseph had encouraged by interpreting his dream, was now out of prison and restored to his position, just as Joseph foretold. He couldn't help but wonder where this would lead.

The answer soon became clear: nowhere. Nothing happened. Days flowed into weeks, weeks into months. Every morning, Joseph wondered if that day would be the day he would hear something.

DIVINE INTERVENTION

How many times have we been there? Our patience runs low as we wait for God to act. Perhaps we even try to manipulate Him so He'll rescue us. But nothing comes of our efforts. We start to realize there's nothing we can do to rush things.

Then God intervenes in a totally unexpected way.

Joseph's hope may have waned, but he faithfully kept doing his duties in prison. Something finally happened, but not until two full years after the cupbearer's release. Yes, twenty-four months later—a long time for a young man in prison to wait.

The guards brought Joseph word: Pharaoh himself wished to see him! "And he was quickly brought from the dungeon. When he had shaved and changed his clothes, he came before Pharaoh."[1]

Suddenly, here was Joseph not only out of prison but standing before Pharaoh. How could this have happened?

MORE DREAMS

It happened because of a chain of events triggered by two perplexing dreams Pharaoh had.

In the first dream, he was standing by the Nile. Rising out from the river came seven cows, "sleek and fat." They were followed by seven ugly, emaciated cows, who ate up the first ones.

Then a second dream: Pharaoh saw seven heads of grain, "healthy and good," growing on one stalk. Then seven other heads of grain sprang up, "thin and scorched by the east wind," and they "swallowed up" the healthy grain.[2]

If you or I had such dreams, we would probably brush them off and forget them. They wouldn't seem threatening or personally applicable, and they aren't nightmares. But in Egypt, dreams were given much weight. The Egyptians believed that the gods spoke to them through dreams, and Egypt's rulers employed specialists

— magicians and wise men — to interpret them.

Pharaoh's parallel dreams troubled him greatly, and the next morning "he sent for all the magicians and wise men of Egypt"[3] to explain the visions. To the credit of these counselors, they admitted they were stumped.

But as the king's cupbearer heard about all this, a light came on for him. He suddenly remembered Joseph. He told Pharaoh the whole story of the dreams that he and the baker had while in prison and how "a young Hebrew" there had correctly interpreted the dreams.

It was worth checking out, "so Pharaoh sent for Joseph." Standing before him, Joseph must have wondered, even feared, what fate was coming his way.

STAYING HONEST AND BOLD

Pharaoh quickly explained the situation. He'd dreamed some things that nobody could interpret. But he'd heard that Joseph could.

In reply to Pharaoh, the first words out of Joseph's mouth sounded like a kiss of death: "I cannot do it"[4] Not an auspicious beginning. Couldn't he at least pretend to help? Who would know he was faking?

How many times have you been in a situation where the easiest way out was to lie or fake it? But a wise supervisor or employer would rather have an honest answer than some wishy-washy version of the truth.

In that first reply to Pharaoh, Joseph added this: "*God* will give Pharaoh the answer he desires."[5] Pharaoh took him up on that. He recounted his dreams to Joseph.

Joseph immediately gave the interpretation, while first emphasizing again the source: "*God* has revealed to Pharaoh what he is
about to do."[6] Joseph said the dreams simply meant that Egypt
would experience seven years of plenty followed by seven years of
famine.

Carefully and authoritatively, Joseph repeated his message: "It
is just as I said to Pharaoh: *God has shown Pharaoh* what he is about
to do. Seven years of great abundance are coming throughout the
land of Egypt, but seven years of famine will follow them."[7]

And why did the dream come in two versions — one with
cows and one with heads of grain? "The reason the dream was
given to Pharaoh in two forms," Joseph said, "is that the matter
has been firmly decided by *God*, and *God* will do it soon." Joseph
again credits his source.

Then Joseph becomes even bolder. He leaves interpreting
and gives a solution to the crisis he's just foretold: Find someone "discerning and wise" and put him in charge of the land.
Joseph further proposes the choosing of commissioners to tax and
manage a fifth of the harvest for the first seven years, storing it as
a reserve for the coming years of famine.[8]

Where did Joseph get such a detailed plan? Obviously it came
from God, for Joseph had no experience or training to prepare
him for this answer.

But what Joseph *did* have was a heart and life prepared to see
God at work, trust His control and guidance, and recognize His
perspective as circumstances unfolded.

READY FOR OPPORTUNITY

As I've observed people whose lives reflect significant position or accomplishment, I wonder, *How did they get to where they are in life? Where and why did they get the opportunity to do what they've done?* I've asked that of my own life.

There are simple yet profound answers. And as we're seeing, Joseph's life illustrates them all.

Plan, but Let God Redirect

Make your plans, but let God change them. "In his heart a man plans his course, but the LORD determines his steps."[9] We set a direction, a path, but God directs us step-by-step, sometimes in a different way than we expect.

That doesn't mean wandering aimlessly or haphazardly through life. We plan. We go in a direction, seeking God's guidance as we do it. "Commit to the LORD whatever you do, and your plans will succeed."[10] We should be praying and planning what we ought to do in the next days, months, and years.

Remember the Source

Remember that all we have is from God. "What do you have that you did not receive? And if you did receive it, why do you boast as though you did not?"[11] Our intellect, our physical appearance, our family, our country of origin, and even our opportunities are all from God. We cannot boast or brag about our abilities or advantages; we're simply responsible for using them well.

Joseph somehow recognized that he was under God's sovereign leading and that his abilities were not of his own making. We too need this healthy balance: knowing we're a product of God's making but keeping a strong sense of responsibility.

Prepare Yourself

None of us knows what future opportunities or challenges will come our way. That's all in God's hands. But the responsibility to prepare is in our hands.

Joseph prepared himself by giving his best to what he was assigned to do. He learned the language, he learned the ways of business and commerce in his new circumstances, and he connected in the community. More important, he guarded his integrity under temptation and trial.

Through education, practice, training, and experience, do all you can to prepare for the future.

Be Faithful

The faithful person is one who can be trusted to do what he says he'll do, to finish a job, to keep his word, to work hard without being watched, to work to the best of his ability, and to be honest. Joseph was all of that. Potiphar and the chief jailer recognized this character trait in Joseph, causing them to give him greater responsibility and authority. It didn't happen all at once. But faithfulness and dependability will always be noticed.

Work Hard

Learning to work hard will pay greater dividends than much of our education. The educated person who doesn't work hard is of little use in the workplace.

In Branson, Missouri, the College of the Ozarks has the nickname "Hard Work U." The students don't pay tuition; instead they work at jobs on campus. They're taught the value of hard work.

Hard work is the polar opposite of laziness. Joseph was such a person. He not only was faithful but also worked hard at what he did.

Take Risks

Taking risks doesn't mean living foolishly; rather, it means standing up for what's right and risking the consequences. It's taking the responsibility for both your successes and your failures. It's seeing an opportunity and moving in that direction, not knowing what the outcome will be. Make decisions on the best information you have and move forward.

Each of these characteristics will launch you on *The Joseph Road* and give you opportunities to seize.

HEARING GOD SPEAK

As I think about the miracles of opportunity Joseph encountered, I'm reminded of the turning points in my own life.

When I entered the United States Air Force, I planned to be a pilot. I was about to finish my training and receive my wings when I failed a formation jet checkride. After a second check, the instructor said, "White, you can fly two-ship formation, but I don't think you'll do well in four-ship formation." With that, I was dismissed from flight training. I later learned there was an overage of pilots and a cut needed to be made.

I was devastated. My plans and dreams were smashed. I then planned to leave the Air Force after my required three years of service.

But God intervened and I was sent to be a mission controller at Cape Canaveral in the fledgling American space program. Suddenly a new door opened.

A few months later, I was talking with a neighbor. I asked him what he planned to do in his next assignment. He said he wanted to teach at the Air Force Academy. When I asked about the requirements for such a position, he mentioned that one needed a master's degree and good grades.

Very rarely in my life have I been able to say, "God told me." But at that point, something happened inside me that I believe was God telling me, "You should get a master's degree and teach at the Air Force Academy." Doing so, I knew, would allow me to be near The Navigators' headquarters and receive further spiritual training in my personal life. As Mary and I talked and prayed, we agreed that we should move forward with that plan.

My next step was to apply to the Air Force to send me to school for a master's degree. They wrote back and said I was well qualified but that they simply didn't send anyone as young as me for a master's degree. We prayed again. We committed to wait one full year—a long time at age twenty-three. I applied again and heard nothing.

DOORS OPENED BY GOD

Meanwhile, I was asked to report to Air Force Systems Command headquarters at Andrews Air Force Base, near Washington, D.C. I didn't know why, and none of my superiors knew what was going on. I flew to Washington and reported to the personnel office at Andrews.

To my surprise, I learned that they wanted me to give a speech. The personnel officer explained about a first-ever Air Force–wide Career Motivation Congress. The topic of how to encourage young officers to stay in the Air Force for a career would be discussed by a gathering of colonels and brigadier generals. "However, they've been senior officers for so long," the personnel officer told me, "that they really don't know what a young person is thinking these days. We would like you to give a speech telling them what a young officer wants out of the Air Force."

I said, "Do you understand I'm not a career officer?"

"Yes," he said.

I asked if I could speak on anything I wish, and he told me that would be fine.

I then mentioned that I had an application somewhere in the system to go to graduate school. "Well," he said, "let's go look for it." He led me to another office, where we found my application in the bottom drawer of a sergeant's desk.

"What's it doing there?" I asked the sergeant.

He explained that it couldn't be approved because I hadn't yet been at my assignment at Cape Canaveral for the required three years.

As the personnel officer and I walked down the hallway, he said he wanted to do something to help me. I told him I really believed that God would lead if anything should be done.

A month later, I returned and gave my speech at the congress. As I walked off the podium, a colonel came up to me and introduced himself as the chief personnel officer at the Air Force Academy. "Lieutenant," he said, "if you'd ever like to teach at the Academy, let me know." I took his card.

Later that day, I went to a formal dinner concluding the conference. After I walked out of the banquet room, an old white-haired colonel came up and said to me, "Lieutenant, I hope you enjoy your school tour." That was the first news I had that I'd been specially approved to attend graduate school.

God opened each of these doors for me, but I had to choose to walk through them. In all likelihood I wouldn't have been asked to give that speech had I not been working hard in the job into which God had thrust me. I worked very hard. Without such preparation, I wouldn't have been eligible or considered for my subsequent assignments.

What have been your own opening doors—your "twists of fate"? How has God surprised you? If you keep your eyes and ears open, you'll see many opportunities open up. They can be as small as your son asking you to come meet his basketball coach and you end up helping to coach. They can be as large as a new job in a new city.

Most often, the opportunity will come when you least expect it—when you're not really looking for something, but you're simply faithfully laboring away day by day at your normal tasks.

Let God produce your "twist of fate."

QUESTIONS FOR REFLECTION

1. As you look back on your life, what events have been sign-posts of God's leading in your life?
2. When you were thrust into circumstances that seemed over-whelming, did you still sense God's leading?

3. How ready and prepared are you to recognize God's control and specific guidance in your unfolding circumstances? Is there anything you need to do to be better prepared?

There are risks and costs to a program of action. But they are far less than the long-range risks and costs of comfortable inaction.

—John F. Kennedy

Look for a discerning and wise man and put him in charge.

—Genesis 41:33

CHAPTER 9

SIGNPOST:
See the Open Doors and Walk Through Them

SEIZING THE OPPORTUNITY

N No human being knows the future—not the next minute, hour, or day, much less next year or years to come. Nor can anyone predict the consequences of their actions or lack of action. As the writer of Ecclesiastes tells us, "When times are good, be happy; but when times are bad, consider: God has made the one as well as the other. *Therefore, a man cannot discover anything about his future.*"[1] We're only human, and we're vulnerable.

Our only certainty about the future is that *God* knows—and He cares and He directs. We can therefore have confidence because we know that God operates with our true best interests in mind.

Before Joseph heard Pharaoh's dream and was given God's interpretation for it, I doubt he had a clue about what would happen in Egypt's future. And after he heard Pharaoh's description of the dream and relayed God's interpretation of it, perhaps everyone else in attendance was in shock or denial. After all, Pharaoh's dreams were the only evidence that what Joseph predicted would even happen.

But Joseph immediately believed what God indeed had communicated. Responding with clear, strategic thinking, Joseph quickly recognized what needed to be done to prepare for the future crisis that had been foretold.

Boldly he laid out his plan. He might get ridiculed for the folly of it. He might even be sent back into prison for his presumption. But really, what did he have to lose? He had no standing and no guarantees.

CONFIDENCE FROM GOD

I can imagine the scene in Pharaoh's throne room. As Joseph finished speaking, there would be a moment of stunned silence. Then, from among the gathered officials and counselors, questions might well arise.

"How did you figure all that out, when our wisest people could not? Why should this be revealed to you and not to them?"

"I understand your skepticism," Joseph would reply. "I can't fully explain *how* I know, but I do. God has spoken to me in the past, and I know when it's Him speaking and not just my own thoughts."

"What kind of proof do you have?"

"None."

"How do you expect us to believe you?"

"I'm only telling you what I see."

However this discussion developed, something—or *some-one*—convinced Pharaoh and those with him to believe this young Hebrew and what he proposed. In the Genesis account, immediately after Joseph revealed his ideas, what we read is this: "The plan seemed good to Pharaoh and to all his officials."[2]

Pharaoh, of course—unlike the others — had known personally the vivid impression of those God-sent dreams. Their clarity and power must have been unlike anything he'd ever witnessed—unlike anything, that is, except the equal forcefulness of Joseph's clear interpretation and the bold plan he urged. There was something common to both the dreams and Joseph's words, and Pharaoh instantly recognized what it was. Pointing to Joseph, he said to his officials, "Can we find anyone like this man, one in whom is *the spirit of God?*"[3] Quite clearly, Pharaoh saw the hand of God on Joseph.

Joseph sensed it too, and that was the source of the confidence he displayed.

FAST CHANGES

Then came Pharaoh's stunning announcement: He made Joseph his prime minister, complete with authority over his key leaders.

Suddenly, Joseph was transformed from a prisoner to Pharaoh's adviser and prime minister. The sequence of events happening next are dizzying in how quickly they changed the life:

- Joseph was given authority over "the whole land of Egypt"[4]

- Pharaoh put his own signet ring of authority on Joseph's finger.
- He put a gold chain of royal authority around Joseph's neck.
- He clothed Joseph in royal attire.
- He paraded Joseph through the streets in a special royal chariot, recognized as that of the second in command in the nation.
- He assigned a squadron of soldiers to "make way" for Joseph's chariot.
- He even gave Joseph an Egyptian name: Zaphenath-Paneah.

At the time, Joseph was thirty years old. For the past thirteen of those years, he'd always been either a slave or a prisoner. Now he'd been brought instantly to the pinnacle of civil authority, with every trapping of power. But in the confidence of his relationship with God, he was ready for it all.

In fact, Joseph's appointment was highly unusual in this country where bloodlines and dynasties were so important. Scholars note a 140-year gap in Egyptian history when they were ruled by foreigners, the Hyksos. It was a dark period in Egyptian history, with almost no records existing. The Hyksos, being foreigners, would be much more open to another foreigner having such a position of power.

Adding to the strangeness was the fact that Pharaoh assigned Joseph a wife: Asenath, the daughter of a high priest who served Egypt's sun god. She was no doubt a pagan worshipper of Egyptian deities. There's no indication of Joseph's question or struggle over accepting this marriage. But what were his choices? In Egypt at that time, we know of no other worshippers of the one true God, the God of Abraham, Isaac, and Jacob.

Although we learn nothing further about Asenath except that she gave birth to Joseph's two sons, Joseph must have won her over to the God of Israel, the one true God. Nevertheless, their first few years together must have been quite interesting for them both.

GOD IS ALWAYS INVOLVED

Can a believer function well—even thrive—in the midst of people and environments and systems that are secular, even ungodly? The big picture of Joseph's life shows us that yes, this is indeed the case.

I recall several events in my life in which God put me in environments with no apparent religious or spiritual support. Growing up, I recall little spiritual climate or practice in our family. My parents had divorced when I was just a few months old, and for the next eight years, I was raised by my mother and her father, my grandfather. This was in a rural Iowa town of a hundred people (our phone number was "9"). I started school there in a one-room schoolhouse.

When my mother remarried, we left my grandfather and moved 1,500 miles away to Spokane, Washington, a city of 180,000; my third-grade classroom there was bigger than my entire school back in Iowa. I had no control over any of these events in my life, yet looking back, I can see God's hand guiding and shaping my life by what I went through.

Years later, when the Air Force sent me to Cape Canaveral

after I failed in pilot training, I was assigned to work with five other mission controllers, none of whom was a believer. This is the norm for most of us. We don't have a warm-fuzzy spiritual environment. The cold reality of a secular world needs the light of the gospel, which should be emanating from our life.

In the midst of those circumstances, in both my early life as well as later, it is clear that God was involved.

LIVING IN A SECULAR ENVIRONMENT

Perhaps you find yourself surrounded by evil and ungodly influences. What should you do?

First, I suggest you take inventory. Recognize the choices that brought you to your current reality. How did you get there? Was it through your own choices? Was it by God's direction? Was it necessary to support your family? Sometimes we choose certain situations out of selfishness, greed, or pride. If you discover that's true for you, confess it and look to Christ for forgiveness. God can certainly overrule even in circumstances of your own making.

Second, step back and see the big picture. Review how God has led you up to this point in your life. Make a list of past key events in your personal history. Especially list those events over which you had no control. Recognize and acknowledge how He has guided you.

Third, determine to renew your personal commitment to walk daily with God regardless of your circumstances. As you do that, you'll be led day by day concerning what you should do.

Fourth, keep applying the lessons of *The Joseph Road*: Prepare yourself, be faithful, work hard, and take risks. You're judged not by how well you thrive on easy tasks but by how you perform in the trials, the hard tasks, the difficult situations.

QUESTIONS FOR REFLECTION

1. What significant doors has God opened to you at this time? What can you do to make the most of these opportunities?
2. How would you describe your level of confidence as you step forward to maximize opportunities? What God-given confidence can you draw upon?
3. What secular environments are common in your life? In the midst of them, how are you demonstrating obedience to God?

Great works are performed not by strength but by perseverance.

—Samuel Johnson

Then Pharaoh told all the Egyptians, "Go to Joseph and do what he tells you."

—Genesis 41:55

CHAPTER **10**

SIGNPOST:
Put Feet on Your Plans — Be a Doer

PRESSING ON

an you imagine the shock of the Egyptian people as they heard the news about the man to whom Pharaoh had just given total charge over their country? Word would have spread like wildfire. (Potiphar and his wife must have shuddered with fear thinking about what Joseph might do to them.)

If we pretend for a moment that Egypt back then had newspapers like ours, the continuing story might have made for fascinating reading in the *Egyptian Gazette*, beginning with this brief item one day:

AN UNKNOWN ON THE RISE?

The royal court is buzzing in response to reports of an unknown person seen riding from the palace yesterday in Pharaoh's number-two chariot, which normally is reserved for use by the senior minister in His Majesty's government.

The unidentified man rode under protection of the palace guard.

Meanwhile, speculation increased that the palace will announce shortly a major administrative appointment.

Then the next day, this front-page headline and report:

EX-HEBREW PRISONER CHOSEN BY PHARAOH AS NEW PRIME MINISTER

In an unprecedented action that staggered court observers, His Royal Highness the Pharaoh has given the position of prime minister to a Hebrew just released from the royal prison.

The new prime minister has been granted the name Zaphenath-Paneah. He was formerly known as Joseph, a servant in charge of the household of Potiphar, though he was later removed from that position and has remained in detention for a number of years.

The palace confirmed that Zaphenath-Paneah's authority throughout all Egypt will be second only to that of Pharaoh himself.

Further details about the reasons for this unprecedented action were not released at this time, and veteran court observers were at a loss to explain it.

PRIME MINISTER GIVES TOP PRIORITY
TO BUILDING VAST NEW STOREHOUSES

In his first public action as Egypt's new prime minister, Zaphenath-Paneah has begun directing the immediate construction of massive storage facilities at several locations throughout the nation.

The palace announced new laws requiring all available labor to be allocated to these facilities, giving them top priority over all other construction, both private and public.

The exact purpose for this vast project and the reason for its urgency were not explained. However, court observers speculated that the storage facilities are intended for grain, as the stated target date for their completion coincides with the beginning of the grain harvest

Then a few months later:

GRAIN HARVEST TO FACE 20 PERCENT TAX

Ending weeks of intense speculation, Prime Minister Zaphenath-Paneah yesterday confirmed that the government will be appropriating a one-fifth share of all Egyptian grain in this year's harvest. He also acknowledged that a nationwide network of commissioners is being assembled to supervise the collecting of the grain.

The grain will be stored in the government's new storage facilities that are nearing completion at several sites throughout the land. The prime minister stated that the vast new storage system is on target for meeting all construction deadlines.

The rise of the storehouses has heightened fears in recent

weeks among many of the nation's landowners. Several of them converged on the palace this week, seeking to meet with authorities to air their concerns.

The prime minister also confirmed that the 20 percent share of grain to be taken from this year's harvest will be held in reserve rather than offered for sale or export.

Then the next day, this front-page headline and report:

BEHIND THE TAX AND STOREHOUSES: ONLY A DREAM?

Reputable sources with inside links to the palace, speaking on strict condition of anonymity, have informed the *Egyptian Gazette* that the surprise appointment of Prime Minister Zaphenath-Paneah—plus his controversial 20 percent tax on grain and the construction of massive facilities for storing it—are all the result of disturbing dreams that Pharaoh reported nearly six months ago.

These sources have disclosed an amazing chain of events in which Zaphenath-Paneah not only interpreted His Majesty's dreams—which the royal magicians and counselors were unable to understand—but also immediately laid out the comprehensive plan for the grain tax and the storehouses.

At the time, Zaphenath-Paneah (known then only as Joseph the Hebrew) was an imprisoned slave. But according to our palace sources, he developed a reputation in prison as an incredibly accurate interpreter of dreams.

He was therefore summoned from prison to the palace on the morning after Pharaoh reported his troubling dreams, which featured cattle, a few stalks of grain, and the Nile River. Although every royal wise man and adviser judged the dreams too puzzling to decipher, the Hebrew prisoner wasted no time unfolding their significance as well as calling for immediate government action in response.

According to our sources, the prophetic meaning of Pharaoh's dreams as perceived by Zaphenath-Paneah — and immediately accepted by Pharaoh and his counselors — is that Egypt will experience several years of abundant harvests followed by a severe, long-term famine.

The following month:

RECORD GRAIN CROP GETS MIXED REACTION

As the grain harvest continues in full swing, reports from every part of Egypt indicate a record-breaking yield far exceeding previous harvests.

But the bumper crop is producing mixed feelings among farmers and landowners. They're obviously pleased with the heightened productivity of their fields, but they find it hard to let go of the 20 percent required by the government's recent grain tax.

As harvest time ended, the following letter appeared on the *Gazette*'s opinion page. It was one of many like it that were published throughout the next seven years.

To the Editor:

As our entire country enjoys the greatest prosperity we've ever known, it's time to respectfully request His Royal Highness the Pharaoh and the royal government to reconsider the oppressive 20 percent grain tax. Think how much further economic development we would see if this grain were sold or exported!

Why pay heed to dire predictions for the future that are impossible to prove and ridiculous to believe? This is no time to give in to frightening dreams. This is a time for *growth*!

Why not repeal the tax and dismantle the storehouses? Let's unleash our prosperity! Let's see how high we can go!

CONTINUED FAITHFULNESS

Many lessons emerge from Joseph's grand strategy: God answers prayers, He opens doors of opportunity, He gives responsibility, and then *we* must act.

Many times we pray for a promotion, business success, or a new job. We're thrilled when it happens. Then the stark realization of responsibility sets in. Joseph's life shows us that there's no "autopilot" for responsibility. Plans need to be made. Hard work must be invested. Extra time is demanded. Nothing's easy or automatic. Performance is now what counts.

The picture that emerges from the Genesis account of this part of Joseph's story continues the same consistent picture we've already seen: He's still faithful as ever to his responsibilities, working hard to fulfill them, and experiencing success. Notice his actions:

Joseph went out from Pharaoh's presence and traveled throughout Egypt. During the seven years of abundance the land produced plentifully. Joseph collected all the food produced in those seven years of abundance in Egypt and stored it in the cities. In each city he put the food grown in the fields surrounding it. Joseph stored up huge quantities of grain, like the sand of the sea; it was so much that he stopped keeping records because it was beyond measure.[1]

During this time, Joseph also fathered two sons, and his names for these boys reveal his big-picture understanding and acknowledgment of God's hand upon his destiny. His firstborn son was Manasseh, the name coming from a Hebrew word meaning "forget," for Joseph said, "It is because *God has made me forget all my trouble* and all my father's household."[2] The second son's name, Ephraim, was derived from the word for "twice-fruitful": "It is because *God has made me fruitful* in the land of my suffering."[3] Joseph was still seeing and acknowledging God's hand in everything.

EVEN WHEN THERE'S OPPOSITION

Setting out in a new direction can bring opposition and criticism. In the midst of prosperous times in Egypt, Joseph carried out a nationwide program of storing away large quantities of grain since he knew what was coming at the end of seven years. This was probably an unpopular plan with many, but Joseph persevered in his plan.

When you believe that you have a word from God or sense His leading, not everyone will agree or understand. Your move to another city disrupts the family. Friends wonder at your choice. Your new job may require personnel changes and reorganization, and someone may be hurt in that process. And as you work hard through personal motivation and necessity, you may risk offending other workers simply by setting a higher standard they don't want to be measured by.

When Mary and I made the decision for me to join The Navigators and leave active duty in the Air Force after almost fourteen years—six years short of a generous retirement—my grandmother cried, our parents wondered, many friends were opposed, and some of my coworkers thought I'd gone off the deep end. Yet we knew this was God's direction. Years later, when I was given an opportunity to become a general in the Air Force Reserves, I knew it would be demanding and hard, although in some ways it also confirmed the validity of decisions I'd made earlier. Because I'd just become president of The Navigators, some questioned my decision to pursue both challenges at the same time. I sacrificed vacations and free time to pull it off. My family paid a price, but it was one we'd agreed to pay. In the Air Force job, I had to perform or not get promoted. In my job with The Navigators, I had to lead in enacting many changes, some of them not well understood by the staff.

In such times, I knew I needed to persevere in the direction God has led us.

THE RIGHT PERSPECTIVE FOR PRESSING ON

In life, there are no shortcuts. When difficult times come, we need to keep engaged and pressing on, even if we don't feel like it.

Know that God placed you where He wants you. Our neighborhood, our schools, and our workplaces reflect God's special calling for us. When we realize that, we develop a totally new perspective on life that frees us. We stop fighting our circumstances. Instead, we begin to look for God's purpose *in* those circumstances.

Realize too that times of testing go hand in hand with God's purposes. But this can be hard to accept. No one wakes up one morning and prays, "God, please send me a serious struggle so I can learn to trust You." We don't look for trials and testing; by nature, we all desire ease and comfort.

When you read the Psalms, you don't find prayers asking for a harsh life or more difficult circumstances in which to trust God; instead, the psalmists plead for deliverance and the courage to persevere. They ask hard questions and even complain. They often reveal personal struggles and the search for understanding. They also show that when God's greater purposes come into focus, it's all part of a learning process. Job realized this when he said of God, "When he has tested me, I will come forth as gold."[4]

Sometimes we see God's purpose while we're right in the midst of trials. More often we see His purpose only in retrospect. There is no evidence that during Joseph's years of slavery and imprisonment that he knew what God was doing or why. Joseph simply had to trust and then act in the midst of his circumstances with faith and integrity.

As I write this, I'm experiencing certain life circumstances that I've pleaded with God to remove. He hasn't. I've experienced times of deep loss and even depression. I've had sleepless nights and fearful, half-awake mornings. So these words are as much for me as for you who read them. I do have confidence that God is doing His work in my life through these difficulties. It's not fun, but it's real. And it has given me a different perspective on all the life successes I've experienced.

Finally, realize that our good times are preparation for the bad times. We've all experienced good times in life—they give us memories and hope when life becomes arduous. They also prepare us for the future—financially, emotionally, educationally. The famous ant illustration from Proverbs says it well:

> You lazy fool, look at an ant.
>> Watch it closely; let it teach you a thing or two.
> Nobody has to tell it what to do.
>> All summer it stores up food;
>> at harvest it stockpiles provisions.
> So how long are you going to laze around doing nothing?
>> How long before you get out of bed?
> A nap here, a nap there, a day off here, a day off there,
>> sit back, take it easy—do you know what comes next?
> Just this: You can look forward to a dirt-poor life,
>> poverty your permanent houseguest![5]

In every area of life, the principle of saving and preparing bears fruit, while spending and debt do not. Whether it's money, emotions, reputation, or relationships, the principle of investing trumps wasting every time.

Don't fool yourself. Get ready for what's next. That's *The Joseph Road*.

QUESTIONS FOR REFLECTION

1. What hard work is particularly needed from you now in order for you to be faithful to what God has called you to?

2. As you've stepped out to obey God in a new direction, what kind of opposition or questioning have you experienced from others?

3. What are the toughest circumstances you're facing in life right now? Are you fighting those circumstances or looking for God's purpose *within* those circumstances?

God has wisely kept us in the dark concerning future events and reserved for himself the knowledge of them, that he may train us up in a dependence upon himself and a continued readiness for every event.

— Matthew Henry

The famine was severe in all the world.

— Genesis 41:57

CHAPTER 11

SIGNPOST:
Keep Focused on God During Adversity

WHEN DISASTER STRIKES, TESTING BEGINS

Back to the *Egyptian Gazette*:

ASTROLOGERS FORESEE ANOTHER GOOD YEAR

With another record-breaking harvest just past — the seventh in a row — there's no end in sight for the current prosperity Egypt is enjoying. Astrologers are predicting still more abundant crops next year.

Meanwhile, hopes are increasing among many land-owners that the hated grain tax will finally be done away with, as government storage facilities are filled to overflowing and Prime Minister Zaphenath-Paneah has confirmed there are no plans for building additional storage.

Some observers have speculated that the government may be forced to begin releasing the stored grain, finally recognizing that the vast storage project was all a big mistake and not wanting to continue being stuck with such a huge surplus. But this has triggered fears among landowners that a sudden market glut caused by a government grain release will only push prices downward to disastrous levels.

Because of the long string of abundant harvests, most landowners have their own gener-

ous stockpiles of grain — more than enough, they say, to make up for a bad crop anytime in the future. They view the government's immense grain supplies as not only unnecessary but also an economic threat.

As one landowner told the *Egyptian Gazette*, speaking on condition of anonymity, "The whole government storehouse scheme was a monstrous blunder from the start. So far we've managed to get by without it causing too much harm, but I'm scared that somehow it's going to eat our lunch in the end."

Several months later, the substance and tone of the news is drastically different:

CROP FAILURE FORECAST WIDENS

As the time of harvest nears, reports from every part of Egypt confirm that disease and drought have all but destroyed this year's crop, an inconceivable

reversal from the overflowing yields of previous years.

Meanwhile crop reports from neighboring countries are no better. Not a single nation is forecasting anything near an ample harvest. The extent of the drought and disease is larger than anything anyone can remember.

Food prices continue to rise, despite assurances from landowners and grain distributors that reserves from record harvests in the past are sufficient to see the country through the coming year.

A year later, the news only gets worse:

FAMINE UNAVOIDABLE; DESPERATION GROWS; PRESSURE INCREASES FOR GOVERNMENT HELP

As disastrous crop forecasts overwhelm the nation for the second straight year, crushing all hopes of a recovery — either in Egypt or anywhere else — the reality is setting in that widespread starvation in the coming year is unavoidable in this country without a government rescue.

Updated reports from landowners indicate that their private surplus reserves, which alone carried the nation through the past difficult year, will not last another one. Many say their supplies are already at or near depletion.

Meanwhile, the government's extensive grain reserves, which have remained securely locked away and heavily guarded, are increasingly seen as the nation's only hope. Crowds assemble daily outside the palace walls, crying out for relief.

A few months later:

GOVERNMENT GRAIN RELEASED FOR SALE

As the international famine continues to worsen, Prime Minister Zaphenath-Paneah announced yesterday the authorized sale of grain from government storehouses. He said the grain will be priced at two levels: the lower price for Egyptians, the higher price for all those coming from other nations to buy grain.

Famines were a fact of Egyptian history. Egypt's agriculture is driven by the annual flooding of the rivers (primarily the Nile), creating the vast, fertile Nile Delta and a rich deposit of soil left by receding floods—as much as seventy feet of accumulated topsoil. The famine was most likely caused by a drought, diminishing the enriching floods and brought farming to a literal standstill.

This was neither the first nor the last time such a famine occurred. For example, nine centuries after the time of Christ, low floodwaters triggered a two-year famine that killed six hundred thousand people. An account of another famine a few centuries later tells of survivors eating human flesh and graves ransacked for food.

It was in the midst of such potential devastation that Egyptians actually welcomed the forceful rule of Zaphenath-Paneah.

WHAT HARD TIMES DO

Hard times reveal the character of people. Soft times foster ease and greed.

Hard times bring out tough-minded leadership. Soft times

breed self-centered, indulgent leadership.

Hard times either turn people to God or drive them away from God.

Throughout Egypt's good times, Joseph had been forcing his policies of building and taxation, although they may have seemed oppressive to many. Now, as the prophesied hard times begin, we'll see Joseph responding with equal toughness. Eventually he will bring the entire nation of Egypt to its knees before Pharaoh as the price they must pay to survive.

On the surface, it may seem in parts of the story that Joseph was insensitive. But consider this: Suppose you're elected as mayor in a moderate-sized city. It has laws and ordinances you didn't create but that you must enforce. In the process, you find you don't like some of the laws or the actions you must take to enforce them. But still you fulfill your responsibility.

Joseph faced that. He had authority, but he was also under authority. He discharged his responsibilities with loyalty to his Egyptian king and with the clear knowledge that he was in the midst of fulfilling God's revealed prophecy to him.

He was on orders from God, via the Pharaoh's dreams, to save lives. Only later did he find that it was saving his own family. With vague memory of his youthful dreams, never again repeated, he was simply fulfilling what he now saw as his destiny.

He just did his job, a difficult one at best. And Zaphenath-Paneah's first responsibility was to preserve the Egyptians.

OUR TIMES OF FAMINE

For us, several *Joseph Road* principles emerge from these years of famine.

One is simply that there will also be times of famine for us, physically and spiritually. At times, our life circumstances will seem out of control: because of the economy, other people's actions, illness, relational conflicts, job difficulties, family disruptions.

With these things comes physical stress as well as spiritual struggles. Recognizing the reality of such times helps us realize we're human and that we're in a spiritual battle.

We should expect such tough experiences to come our way. "Dear friends, do not be surprised at the painful trial you are suffering, as though something strange were happening to you."[1] Or, as Eugene Peterson paraphrases it in *The Message*,

> Friends, when life gets really difficult, don't jump to the conclusion that God isn't on the job. Instead, be glad that you are in the very thick of what Christ experienced. This is a spiritual refining process, with glory just around the corner.

Another principle from the famine times: When you have authority, exercise it well and faithfully, as Joseph did.

Authority is never to be taken lightly, especially in the midst of difficult times. All of us have some authority, even if it's just in our family. Many have authority at work, at church, or in some level of political structure. In exercising that authority, our decisions may not always be popular.

Disaster and times of testing bring out the best and worst in people. Some work to preserve themselves. Others work to serve and help others, even when they themselves are under stress. As we will see later, it brought out the worst in his brothers. It brought out the best in Joseph, particularly in his leadership and character.

QUESTIONS FOR REFLECTION

1. What benefits in your life are you experiencing now because of hard times you've had to go through in the past?
2. What have hard times revealed about your own character?
3. What kinds of authority do you currently have? What would other people say about how well you're exercising this authority?

Man is unjust, but God is just; and finally justice triumphs.

— HENRY WADSWORTH LONGFELLOW

Do this and you will live, for I fear God.

— GENESIS 42:18

CHAPTER **12**

SIGNPOST:
You're the Hand of God

THE GAME BEGINS

Times were desperate. The famine was all-encompassing, afflicting nation after nation.

Word spread quickly that one place still had food. And one man there—Joseph—was in the spotlight: "All the countries came to Egypt to buy grain *from Joseph*, because the famine was severe in all the world."[1]

Mirroring the plight of countless families in all these lands, Jacob and his family took desperate action as well. When "Jacob learned that there was grain in Egypt,"[2] he sent ten of his sons—all except young Benjamin, Joseph's only full-brother —to Egypt to buy food. His father was fearful of losing him as he lost Joseph. His words to them prefigure a deeper theme that Joseph himself will later articulate: "Go down there and buy some for us, so *that we may live and not die.*"[3]

At least Jacob's family was wealthy enough to pay for the grain they hoped to purchase. Still, there was no guarantee, as Zaphenath-Paneah's first responsibility was to preserve the Egyptians by selling grain to them.

THE GOVERNOR

Joseph's story now reaches a major crossroads.

Thirteen years of deprivation, mistreatment, and injustice in Joseph's life had been followed by years of unimagined power. At this point, we don't yet see clues that he'd figured out the ultimate purpose for all these strange events in his life. But he was grateful for where the events had brought him, and he took his responsibility seriously. In this time of deepening crisis, he was the ultimate go-to person, as the account in Genesis emphasizes: "Joseph was the governor of the land, the one who sold grain to all its people."[4]

His responsibility included the approval of grain sales to foreigners, as caravans poured in from surrounding countries. One day, among these foreigners who approached him, Joseph recognized his own brothers.

What happens in the remainder of the Genesis account represents one of the most fascinating and intriguing stories in all of Scripture.

"When Joseph's brothers arrived, they bowed down to him with their faces to the ground."[5] With that, there must have come to Joseph the sudden remembrance—like a lightning bolt from heaven—of those dreams so long ago about his brothers bowing before him.

"Although Joseph recognized his brothers, they did not recognize him."[6] The manner, appearance, and dress of this all-powerful man was nothing like that of the teenager they last saw when they betrayed their brother so long ago. Plus, Joseph did nothing to disclose his identity; "he pretended to be a stranger." Thus began what seems almost like a game that Joseph plays with his brothers — one that involves intensifying complications as it unfolds.

HARSH ENCOUNTER

What would you have done in Joseph's shoes?

We can easily imagine other directions in which this story might have gone. Joseph could have immediately revealed himself to his brothers and shown anger for what they had done to him long ago. His revenge could have taken many terrible forms, given his powerful position. On the other hand, while revealing himself, he might also have made clear right away that he forgave them.

Joseph took neither of those paths. Instead, we read that while hiding his identity, he "spoke harshly to them." After asking where they were from, he bluntly accused them four times of being spies and then "put them all in custody for three days."[7]

We tend to want to criticize Joseph's ruthlessness here or at least question it. Had he simply decided to teach his brothers a lesson by manipulating the further consequences of their earlier misdeeds?

The intricate way this complex story is put together in Genesis helps us answer this question. For example, immediately prior to his first accusation, we read these words regarding Joseph: "Then *he remembered his dreams* about them."[8] We're being alerted to the fact that Joseph is seeing this new encounter with his brothers in a larger, divine perspective reflected by those long-ago dreams, and it's a perspective that far transcends any thought of personal revenge. It was those God-given dreams—not his brothers' evil actions—that were in the driver's seat of Joseph's response.

We also see larger forces at work in the brothers' responses triggered by Joseph's actions. They testify that they "are honest men," and this honesty brings out their statement that they're a family of twelve brothers, not just ten: The youngest was at home with their father, "and *one is no more*."⁹

At that moment, it would have been easy and natural for them not to mention the young brother still at home; there was no real need to do so (as their sorrowful father, Jacob, would later point out to them in dismay).

It would also have been easy for them not to mention the long-lost other brother, but this troubling confrontation they were having with Egypt's governor somehow kept bringing Joseph to their minds.

In response, Joseph's treatment grew even harsher. With a solemn oath in Pharaoh's name, he vowed, "You will not leave this place unless your youngest brother comes here."¹⁰ He decided to put their honesty to the test: One of them must go and fetch the youngest brother while the others remain imprisoned in Egypt. To underline his seriousness and give them time to think it over he had them all locked up.

GUILT REVEALED

Three days later, the governor brought out the brothers and spoke to them again. He now modified his demand: Only one of them need stay behind in prison while the others went to Canaan to bring back the youngest brother.

While stating this, the governor pointedly brought God into the picture: "I fear God," he told them. He also expressed the brothers' situation in life-and-death terms: "Do this and you will live . . . that you may not die."[11]

These words brought another revealing response from the brothers. They spoke among themselves in Hebrew, unaware that this harsh Egyptian governor could fully understand them.

Because of their guilty consciences, their lost brother, Joseph, had stayed in their thoughts. They now expressed a direct cause-and-effect between their evil treatment of him and their own present troubles, as they confessed essentially to murdering him: "Surely we are being punished *because of our brother*. We saw how distressed he was when he pleaded with us for his life, but we would not listen; *that's why this distress has come upon us*."[12] All these years, Joseph's pleas for mercy had haunted them — the pleas they refused to hear at the time. Since then, they had lived with ruined consciences and the lack of inner peace, for they had refused to confess the truth to their father, choosing instead to deliberately keep up their deception.

Now Reuben's words against them reflected the depths of a guilt they could not escape: "Didn't I tell you not to sin against the boy? But you wouldn't listen! *Now we must give an accounting for his blood*."[13]

Hearing their confession, Joseph was overcome: "He turned away from them and began to weep."[14] His emotions were deep, his tears a sure indication that he had already forgiven them, even to the point of sympathizing with their torment over their sin against him.

But the governor had to maintain the harsh exterior. He "turned back and spoke to them again. He had Simeon taken from them and bound before their eyes."[15]

The other nine brothers started back to Canaan with their sacks full of grain. Despite their uncertainty over Simeon's fate, they might well have breathed a sigh of relief after finally leaving the Egyptian governor's presence.

But Joseph's game with them was far from over.

WHAT HAS GOD DONE?

When they stopped for the night, one of them discovered that his silver intended as payment for the grain was in his sack.

Despair kicked in. "Their hearts sank and they turned to each other trembling"[16]; far more than they knew, their words to each other pointed to the essential truth behind all these bewildering experiences: "What is this that *God has done to us*?"[17]

Continuing on to Canaan (rather than going back to Joseph to return the silver), they explained to their father all that had transpired, including the governor's demand that Benjamin be taken back. Then, plunging them deeper into fear, they discovered the rest of their silver in the other sacks.

By now, Jacob's anguish was even greater than theirs. He cried out to his sons, "You have deprived me of my children. Joseph is no more and Simeon is no more, and now you want to take Benjamin. *Everything is against me!*"[18]

Amazingly, by naming Joseph here in his charge that the brothers had deprived him of his "children," Jacob's words hinted that he knew more than the brothers had suspected about their responsibility for Joseph's disappearance. Hearing this, they would have been freshly reminded of their guilt.

This moment may well have been the low point of Jacob's long life. Ironically, his anguish was not only the result of having been deceived by his older sons about Joseph's fate but also an indirect result of how the brothers themselves were deceived by Joseph, the son Jacob loved most. Was the old man now reaping the consequences of his own past?

Jacob's name means "he deceives," and deception had been a pattern of his life. It was especially evident when he conspired with his mother to deceive his father, Isaac, thereby robbing Esau of their father's paternal blessing in order to receive it for himself.[19] With two wives and two concubines, Jacob had set up a family based on conflict and deceit.

Battered by the lingering consequences of those actions, Jacob now operated out of fear, steadfastly refusing to even consider sending Benjamin to Egypt. But as the famine became worse and all the grain they'd bought in Egypt was used up, Jacob was forced to reconsider. To help him reach that point, his son Judah pledged his own life if anything happened to Benjamin.[20]

Jacob had the brothers take special gifts for the governor, along with double the amount of silver.[21] His parting words to them reflected the tension between his faith in God and a fear that led to resignation:

Take your brother also and go back to the man at once. And *may God Almighty grant you mercy before the man* so that he will let your other brother and Benjamin come back with you. As for me, if I am bereaved, I am bereaved.[22]

Mercy from God Almighty was indeed what Jacob and his entirely family would soon become aware of, flowing toward them through their son and brother, the servant of God and governor of Egypt.

But the game Joseph was playing still had plenty more moves to come.

As you reflect on Joseph's realization of God's purpose, can you look back and see God's hand and wisdom in the events of your life? You are as much a fulfillment of God's purposes as Joseph was. You may not save a nation, but you will deeply impact the lives of your family and those you love. Stop for a moment and ask God to reveal to you the purpose of the past years of your life.

QUESTIONS FOR REFLECTION

1. How would you describe Joseph's actions as he finally encountered his brothers again after all those years away from them? What do you think was uppermost in Joseph's mind at this time?
2. What are the strongest character qualities you see in Joseph in this part of his story?
3. What are the strongest character qualities you see in Joseph's brothers in this part of the story?

He who commits injustice is ever made more wretched than he who suffers it.

— PLATO

May God Almighty grant you mercy before the man.

— GENESIS 43:14

CHAPTER 13

SIGNPOST:
See God in All the Details

THE GAME ENDS

rriving again in Egypt, the brothers were surprised and frightened to be summoned to the governor's house, not yet knowing that the occasion was a feast.

They assumed the worst: "He wants to attack us and overpower us and seize us as slaves."[1] They'd had enough experience with this man to realize that nothing enjoyable could come from closer exposure to him.

STILL HIDDEN

Taking Joseph's steward aside, they explained with full honesty the situation regarding the money they found earlier in their sacks. It was all some mistake! Now they had brought all that money back with them, plus more to buy additional grain. They insisted, "We don't know who put our silver in our sacks."[2]

The steward's response was puzzling and troubling: "It's all right. . . . Don't be afraid. *Your God, the God of your father*, has given you treasure in your sacks; I received your silver."[3]

The steward apparently had been in on Joseph's game all along. Moreover, from these words we get a glimpse of Joseph's influence on those he led. How could this steward have known about their God, the one God of their father Jacob — the one true God — unless Joseph had talked openly about Him?

After being led to the governor's house, the brothers learned to their astonishment that they would be dining there. Instead of being forced to serve as slaves, they themselves would be served. Was this some kind of trap?

Joseph soon joined them. Once more, "they bowed down before him to the ground," a reminder again of Joseph's long-ago dreams. With a courteousness in stark contrast to his previous harshness, the governor inquired about their father's health. They gave a good report of Jacob and then "bowed low" before Joseph yet again. It was almost as if Joseph was fully known to them and they were all there simply for a brotherly visit.

At this point, Joseph got his first good look at Benjamin — "his brother Benjamin, his own mother's son." Joseph turned to him and blessed him: "God be gracious to you, my son."[4] Like the steward's words to the brothers earlier, here was another pointer to God from an unexpected source.

Joseph was "deeply moved at the sight of his brother." Not yet ready to reveal himself, he was forced by these emotions to leave their presence once more: "Joseph hurried out and looked for a place to weep. He went into his private room and wept there."[5] He was hiding not only his identity but also the depths of his genuine feelings for his family.

As the banquet proceeded, more surprises were in store. The brothers found themselves seated in birth order "and they looked at each other in astonishment." Plus, Benjamin was given five times as much food as the others. "They feasted and drank freely with him."[6]

Even with these clues, they still didn't catch on to Joseph's game.

We're like that too, aren't we? God gives us many clues regarding His direction for us and His control over the issues of our lives, but we miss their meaning.

EVERYTHING AGAINST THEM

The next morning, the brothers started on their return journey to Canaan, their sacks again filled with the precious grain. As they departed, they surely remarked to one another about how different the mood and circumstances were compared to the last time they journeyed away from that place. The fear and distress over the governor's harsh treatment last time were replaced now by pleasant memories of an astonishing feast with him. And far more important, this time all eleven brothers were reunited, all on their way home together to their waiting father.

Suddenly, the next tactic in Joseph's game jarred them more than ever.

They looked back to see Joseph's steward approaching their caravan. His words came like a jolt: "Why have you repaid good with evil?"[7] Later this theme of good and evil would reappear powerfully in a climactic, closure-bringing encounter between Joseph and the brothers, but at that moment, this was still far, far away.

The steward charged the brothers with stealing silver and gold from the governor, including his personal drinking cup, made of silver.

They were incensed at such an accusation. "Far be it from your servants to do anything like that! We even brought back to you from the land of Canaan the silver we found inside the mouths of our sacks. So why would we steal silver or gold from your master's house?"[8] Confident of their innocence, they made an impulsive vow: "If any of your servants is found to have it, *he will die*; and the rest of us will become my lord's slaves"[9]

The steward, perhaps following Joseph's instructions, gave them far better terms but a dreadful outcome nevertheless: "Whoever is found to have it will become my slave; the rest of you will be free from blame."[10]

They quickly let their sacks be searched, eldest to youngest. One by one, the sacks were opened and the grain fingered through. To their alarm, each sack yielded their grain-payment money, which Joseph had directed his servants to put there.

As the youngest, Benjamin's sack was last. Inside was not only the money but also the governor's silver cup.

Now, because of their vow, they were trapped. In shock and utter dejection, "they tore their clothes," exactly as their father Jacob had done decades before when they let him think his son Joseph had been killed.

"They all loaded their donkeys and returned to the city."[11] There was nothing else to do. They couldn't simply let Benjamin be left behind alone, like Simeon last time. If they showed up at home without Benjamin, it would kill their father. They had no choice but to go back and share Benjamin's fate.

Perhaps a couple of them were clinging to the faintest hope of some miracle of deliverance. More likely they all felt as their father did after their first return from Egypt: *Everything is against us*.

Joseph's game was playing out to perfection. As he waited patiently for the steward to bring his brothers back into his presence, it seems likely that he now fully comprehended the role God had given him regarding his family.

He was pushing his brothers into the final stage of this incredible drama. Now, more clearly than ever, we see that what Joseph sought was not revenge but their repentance.

DESPERATE PLEAS

Appearing before the governor, the brothers "threw themselves to the ground before him,"[12] the dream scene repeated yet again.

Under the governor's questioning, Judah took the lead in responding. His drawn-out words portrayed the brokenness settling upon them all: "What can we say to my lord? . . . What can we say? How can we prove our innocence?" He could come to only one conclusion: *"God has uncovered your servants' guilt."*[13] Once again, as happens so often in this biblical narrative of Joseph's life, what is stated has far more divine meaning than the speaker realizes.

Continuing to speak, Judah maneuvered on behalf of Benjamin. He suggested that all the brothers become Joseph's slaves, not just Benjamin alone.

The governor refused, insisting that only Benjamin stay

behind, with the rest free to return "to your father." Such a situation mirrored what had happened decades before: the younger brother sold as a slave to Egypt, the rest returning home to Jacob.

In desperation, Judah boldly stepped closer to the governor. He spoke at length, earnestly emphasizing the value to their father of Benjamin—this "young son born to him in his old age. *His brother is dead*, and he is the only one of his mother's sons left, and his father loves him."[14]

In his lengthy pleading, Judah could not keep from telling the governor more about that lost brother—the one he described as "dead." Judah quoted what their father had said about him: "My wife bore me two sons. *One of them went away from me*, and I said, *'He has surely been torn to pieces.'* And I have not seen him since."[15]

This was likely the first hint Joseph had of how his brothers deceived their father after selling him into slavery. Judah was still repeating that lie. In essence he was lying again, before God and before Joseph, further increasing his own guilt along with that of the brothers huddled behind him.

Hearing this, and imagining his beloved father's agony because of the lie they had concocted, would Joseph now yield to revenge?

Judah went on to repeat Jacob's warning that if the brothers let any harm come to Benjamin, they would bring their father "down to the grave in misery."[16] Judah's words continued to intensify as he pleaded on behalf of this old man "whose life is closely bound up with the boy's life."[17] Finally, in mounting anguish, Judah offered to take Benjamin's place as the governor's slave if he would only release the youngest brother. One final time he spoke for Jacob's sake: "Do not let me see the misery that would come upon my father."[18]

STRAIGHT TALK

These urgent pleadings, with the repeated appeal to protect their father from a broken heart, finally broke Joseph. He "could no longer control himself."[19] He ordered all his Egyptian attendants to leave. Then his voice erupted in tearful cries: "He wept so loudly that the Egyptians heard him."[20]

"I am Joseph!" he told the brothers.

Understandably, they were speechless; "they were terrified at his presence," as they should have been. Now they knew real fear. They were totally exposed in all their sin and deceitfulness.

Joseph urged them closer, which they no doubt perceived as a command they dare not disobey. Reluctantly, with trembling knees, they approached.

He spoke again, telling it straight: "I am your brother Joseph, *the one you sold into Egypt!*"

And if that revelation weren't shock enough, his care and concern for them now overflowed, all with an overarching focus on *God's sovereignty* and *God's salvation*:

Now, do not be distressed and do not be angry with yourselves for selling me here, because *it was to save lives that God sent me ahead of you.* For two years now there has been famine in the land, and for the next five years there will not be plowing and reaping. But *God sent me ahead of you* to preserve for you a remnant on earth and *to save your lives by a great deliverance.*[21]

Here were his hateful, deceitful brothers, who had caused him years of trials, imprisonment, and deprivations. Yet in all of it, Joseph perceived *God* and *God's purposes.*

When Joseph identified himself to them as "the one you sold into Egypt," the brothers' crime against him was in sharp focus. But now Joseph quickly added this: "So then, it was not you who sent me here, but God."[22] *Not you, but God.*

Just as Joseph had quickly discerned God's directing hand in the dreams of Pharaoh, so now he saw the same hand at work in all that had happened within his own family.

This is *The Joseph Road*: to experience and endure injustice and disaster and then see *God* in all of it.

TRUSTING GOD ISN'T EASY

When our difficult circumstances are caused by impersonal factors such as natural disasters or disease, trusting God is easier. But when our suffering is directly caused by other people who act with malice and evil intent, that's quite another matter.

For many of us, the most difficult aspect of faith is trusting in God's loving sovereignty. We often find it hard to fully accept what's being said in such verses as these:

> The LORD does whatever pleases Him,
>> in the heavens and on the earth.[23]

> I am the LORD, and there is no other.
> I form the light and create darkness,
>> I bring prosperity and create disaster;
>> I, the LORD, do all these things.[24]

We can debate this in theory and theology, but only the one who wrestles with these issues in his own life will be able to grasp the significance of God's sovereignty and the comfort. Then we can identify with these words:

For you, O God, tested us;
    you refined us like silver.
You brought us into prison
    and laid burdens on our backs.
You let men ride over our heads;
    we went through fire and water,
    but you brought us to a place of abundance.[25]

Even when we understand and believe this, living out its truth is seldom easy.

Mary and I were tested like this when our only son, Stephen, was brutally murdered on the job. We described our feelings and thoughts to friends in these words:

This reality brings us face-to-face with ultimate questions. "Where was God when this happened? Was he not protecting as we have so often prayed?" It is in this terrible time that we "put up or shut up" in terms of our faith. Is God sufficient? Nothing has changed. Yet everything has changed. Nothing has changed because God is changeless. God is changeless, "the same, yesterday, today and forever." Yet everything has changed because a large part of our lives has been removed. Everything in the human realm is changed because there is an empty place in our hearts and lives. Life will return to normal, yet nothing will ever be normal again. We believe God will bring justice to pass in His time. God will bring good from this terrible event. He will cause many to rethink their lives, priorities—and ultimately their relationship to God.

(The murderer was found, confessed, and was convicted and now is serving fifty-six years in prison. We pray often for his salvation.)

The Joseph Road is neither simple nor easy, but it's God's way.

HOW WE'RE TESTED

Joseph had one perspective; his brothers had another. Having been tested and proven by adversity and injustice, Joseph had been gifted with seeing God's perspective and with making decisions and exercising responsibility as a tool of God's grace.

The brothers were tested by the consequences of their actions, but they mostly failed that test. Yet in His grace and mercy, God was still working to open their eyes and lead them into better things.

This part of Joseph's story touches on a number of ways in which we too are tested in life.

Confession is necessary to begin the process of restoration and healing. We need to clearly acknowledge to God what we've done that has brought us into adverse circumstances.

Our *truthfulness* is often tested. We need to be truthful to God, ourselves, and others. Nothing can remain hidden.

We also need to *recognize the clues* of what God is doing in our lives. God isn't hiding from us nor is He hiding the way out.

But we must perceive, see, and understand the working of God to bring us closer to Himself.

We must also *understand the danger* of remaining unreconciled both with God and with others.

The consequences of our actions are certain, whether in this life or the next of judgment: "He will bring to light what is hidden in darkness and will expose the motives of men's hearts."[26] Ultimate judgment is promised: "We must all appear before the judgment seat of Christ, that each one may receive what is due him for the things done while in the body, whether good or bad."[27] No one gets away with anything. This is no idle threat.

Especially significant is the test of brokenness. Until we're truly broken before God, we won't be able to walk *The Joseph Road*.

QUESTIONS FOR REFLECTION

1. What do you think about this "game" Joseph played with his brothers? What do you think motivated him to respond the way he did?
2. In what ways has God tested you in your past? In what ways is He continuing to test you?
3. What are significant ways you've had to live with consequences of unwise actions in your past?
4. How and when did Joseph acknowledge God's sovereignty? What do you think he wrestled with in terms of his view of God?

Not until we have become humble and teachable, standing in awe of God's holiness and sovereignty . . . acknowledging our own littleness, distrusting our own thoughts, and willing to have our minds turned upside down, can divine wisdom become ours.

—J. I. PACKER

Do not be afraid to go down to Egypt.

—GENESIS 46:3, (GOD'S MESSAGE TO JACOB.)

CHAPTER 14

BROKENNESS, RESCUE, AND REUNION

At this point in Joseph's story, we might be tempted to conclude, "They lived happily ever after." But that's in fairy tales. This is real life, with real people and real consequences.

This is a crossroads not only in the life of Joseph but also in the life of the people of Israel. For the moment, they were rescued from the killer famine, but they were unaware that four hundred years in slavery would come before their descendants returned again to Canaan.

Many of us come to such crossroads in our lives. We've gone through difficult times and now see our way to a better future. But along the way, we've experienced bitterness and brokenness, which colors or poisons all we do.

Joseph is now poised to offer hope and a new life to his family. As we follow the story, let's pause first to examine the place of brokenness in Joseph's life and the life of his father and brothers.

TRUE BROKENNESS

Joseph's brokenness came through his journey from being an indulged, somewhat arrogant child to experiencing betrayal, slavery, success, unjust imprisonment, and finally elevation to power. His brothers' brokenness came involuntarily through sins exposed and confessed. Perhaps they'd never before been broken before God.

Brokenness means being forcibly fractured, shattered, fragmented, routed, subdued, and humbled. King David learned about brokenness after his sin with Bathsheba, shown when he prayed,

> You do not delight in sacrifice, or I would bring it;
>> you do not take pleasure in burnt offerings.
> The sacrifices of God are a broken spirit;
>> a broken and contrite heart,
>> O God, you will not despise.[1]

God wants true brokenness, not just a formulized ritual of confession when we're caught in sin. This is reflected in these words from Paul:

> Now I am happy, not because you were made sorry, but because your sorrow led you to repentance. For you became sorrowful as God intended. . . . Godly sorrow

brings repentance that leads to salvation and leaves no regret, but worldly sorrow brings death.[2]

There's a profound difference between being brokenhearted and being broken before God. When we're caught in sin (adultery, anger, or some other failure), we can be deeply distressed yet not deeply repentant. We can be publicly humiliated yet still be proud in spirit. Being remorseful when we've been exposed isn't the same as being broken before God.

True brokenness is a sacrifice. It involves giving up. It means surrendering our right to be bitter and angry, even in the face of injustice. That is *The Joseph Road*.

How does this true brokenness come about? In Psalm 51, David gives these insights:

- Sensitivity to truth: "Surely you desire truth in the inner parts." Truth is total honesty with God. No excuses. No quibbling.
- Learning God's wisdom: "You teach me wisdom in the inmost place." Wisdom is knowing ourselves in respect to God.
- Being cleansed and washed: "Cleanse me with hyssop, and I will be clean; wash me, and I will be whiter than snow." Hyssop was used to clean sacred places and is still known today as a cleansing agent. Brokenness involves a cleansing from our sin, accomplished only by God. It's His forgiveness that cleanses. (I like verse 7 in *The Message*: "Soak me in your laundry and I'll come out clean, scrub me and I'll have a snow-white light.")

- The result of this process—joy, gladness, and wholeness: "Let me hear joy and gladness; let the bones you have crushed rejoice." We experience a great peace when we finally allow God to break us and rebuild our lives.

THE BROKENNESS GOD WANTS

I remember one of my first lessons in broken things. When I was eleven years old, I became angry with Mother when I couldn't get my way. I picked up my favorite toy and threw it against the wall, irreparably breaking it. I could now understand the nursery rhyme about Humpty Dumpty's "great fall" and being shattered beyond repair. Both children and adults experience the rhyme's truth in our lives. We suffer the consequences of adultery, alcohol abuse, gluttony, bitterness, and anger, knowing we cannot fully put life back together. This is human brokenness.

But it's not the brokenness God wants in our lives.

In his excellent book *Embracing Brokenness* (to which I'm greatly indebted for much in this study), Alan E. Nelson writes this:

> Brokenness is the emptying of selfish ambition so that we are willing and able to be filled with God's spirit. . . . Brokenness, voluntary or involuntary, requires that we release a grip on a certain area of our life.[3]

Much of our experience in brokenness results from involuntary circumstances—illness, failure, family issues, marriage conflicts, the death of those close to us, natural disasters, accidents, or the impact of sin (ours and others).

When we respond to God in true brokenness, we experience what David prays for:

Create in me a pure heart, O God,
    and renew a steadfast spirit within me.
Do not cast me away from your presence
    or take your Holy Spirit from me.
Restore to me the joy of your salvation
    and grant me a willing spirit, to sustain me.[4]

We experience:

- *A pure heart* — purity of motive in life, a clear conscience.
- *A steadfast spirit* — good motivation and attitude, steadfastness.
- *Restored joy* instead of sadness, regret, and depression.
- *A willingness* to obey and follow God.

From godly brokenness, we develop:

- *Humility* — the breaking of our pride.
- *Empathy* — the breaking of our self-centeredness.
- *Submission* — the breaking of our tendency to grasp for control. (Nelson comments that "this control factor is important to understanding brokenness. We often experience breaking in areas where we think we have control.")
- *Faith and letting go* — the breaking of our feeling trapped by not knowing the outcome of our choices.

We may think this task of brokenness is too difficult, but we haven't known true difficulty until God begins to work in us to break our unyielding resistance toward what He's attempting to do in our lives.

RESISTING BROKENNESS

If we resist brokenness before God, there are many negative results —something Joseph's ten brothers learned the hard way. They illustrate well the consequences of sin and resisting brokenness.

- They spent years deceiving their father, living a lie every day, damaging their consciences.
- They lost any joy in the family, as they saw their father grieve and still play favorites with Benjamin.
- They were in constant conflict with each other.
- When they met difficulties in Egypt, they rightly assumed that God was punishing them.
- Even under the pressure of having to bring Benjamin back to Egypt, they still kept their dirty secret about Joseph, again risking their father's well-being.

By contrast, Joseph's brokenness was apparent in the way he responded to adversity. His submission to God's sovereignty and his bold acknowledging of the one true God showed his willingness to accept his lot in life. This was true in his life even when he didn't understand the "why" of it all. And even after he'd become a ruler in Egypt with almost total power, his brokenness showed as he wept for his family.

A PLAN FOR RESCUE AND REUNION

Returning to that moment when Joseph finally revealed himself to his brothers, recall how the brothers were terrified as the shocking reality of Joseph's identity took hold in their awareness. They were facing not just an unpredictable and all-powerful foreign ruler but also a brother they had greatly offended. They had betrayed him and lied about him to his loving father. Now those sins were fully uncovered.

Because their brother was so powerful, would he seek vengeance? They couldn't know his heart; all they knew was their own deceitfulness. And when they heard Joseph's "God sent me" speech, it must have been beyond their comprehension.

Joseph's next words reveal again his strength as a leader, for in light of his family's predicament, he'd formulated an effective plan for their future. The brothers were to take this message from him to Jacob, their father:

This is what your son Joseph says: . . . Come down to me; don't delay. You shall live in the region of Goshen and be near me—you, your children and grandchildren, your flocks and herds, and all you have. I will provide for you there, because five years of famine are still to come.[5]

Then came the magnanimous act: He not only embraced Benjamin and wept but he also "kissed all his brothers and wept over them."[6]

Pharaoh was informed about Joseph's brothers, and because he respected Joseph so highly, he told him, "Bring your father and your families back to me. I will give you the best of the land of Egypt and you can enjoy the fat of the land."[7] He added, "The best of all Egypt will be yours."

So Joseph sent his brothers home to bring back their father. He sent them with food, new clothes, money, and "ten donkeys loaded with the best things of Egypt." Knowing his brothers well, he also commanded them, "Don't quarrel on the way!"[8]

When they arrived in Canaan and began telling their father about Joseph, "Jacob was stunned; he did not believe them." He was convinced only after they carefully explained everything Joseph had said and after he'd seen "the carts Joseph had sent to carry him back." His spirit "revived," and he announced, "My son Joseph is still alive. I will go and see him before I die."[9]

At this point, did the brothers fully confess to Jacob their treachery against Joseph and their lies to their father? The Genesis narrative doesn't say they did. They probably continued their deceit, allowing Jacob to believe that somehow Joseph had escaped disaster on that day so long ago when they showed him Joseph's torn and bloody robe. Jacob may have learned the truth only later in Egypt, from Joseph himself.

Meanwhile, Jacob received a word from God. Setting out for Egypt, he stopped to offer sacrifices to God at Beersheba. There God spoke to him "in a vision at night":

"Jacob! Jacob!"

"Here I am," he replied.

"I am God, the God of your father," he said. "Do not be afraid to go down to Egypt, for I will make you into a great nation there. I will go down to Egypt with you, and

I will surely bring you back again. And Joseph's own hand will close your eyes."[10]

From this encounter with God, Jacob received a promise for the present, for the end of his life, and for his descendents. Four hundred years would pass before all of this was completely fulfilled, but for now, Jacob knew that in these strange circumstances and events, God had determined a bigger purpose.

With the arrival in Egypt of Jacob and the brothers and their families, the rescue was accomplished. The reunion moved everyone to tears. Joseph "threw his arms around his father and wept for a long time."[11]

LOOKING BACK

Only in retrospect can we see the how and why of God's leading in our lives.

I suggest you take time to write down some of the key events in your life, both good and bad, and see for yourself how God has led you. It will give you a basis for thanksgiving and understanding.[12]

If Joseph had looked back on his life and written such a list, it might look like this:

- New coat. I'm my father's favorite. Brothers jealous.
- Two dreams. Now I know what they meant.
- Sold by brothers. Changed my entire life.
- Sold to Potiphar. A hard new life in Egypt.
- False accusations in jail. Decided to keep doing good.
- Interpreting dreams. Again, I heard from God.

- Pharaoh's dream. Clearly God is at work. Why?
- Encountering brothers again. God's purpose is becoming clear.

Looking back on my life, I started my own list:

- Parents divorced when I was an infant.
- Raised by my mother and grandfather in a town of a hundred people in Iowa.
- After my mother's remarriage, moved to Spokane, Washington.
- Refused to attend school for the entire seventh grade.
- At age thirteen, met my natural father.
- In high school, suddenly became a good student.
- Influenced by my history teacher Louis Livingston (who recently died at age 107).
- Walt Nelson—also a presence in my life to this day—helped me consciously receive Christ as Savior.
- As a freshman at the University of Washington, became involved with The Navigators.
- Mentored by businessman Bob Shepler, who was an influence for Christ for the rest of my life.
- Met and married Mary.
- Entered the Air Force and when I failed at the end of pilot training.
- Assigned to Cape Canaveral and involvement as a mission controller in America's new space program.
- Selected to teach at the Air Force Academy.
- Became president of The Navigators.

- Promoted to brigadier general in the Air Force Reserves.
- Our son, Stephen, died.

This is just a partial list. With each one, there was joy or pain or lack of understanding or even anxiety and challenge to my faith. Each event has a longer story behind it, plus a challenge to continue to walk what I'm calling *The Joseph Road*. At each point, I had choices to make and an attitude to nurture, even when I was unsure of why a certain event was happening. Sometimes I chose and reacted well; sometimes I didn't.

With each event you record on your list, make a note of how God used it in your life. For some of the events, you may want to record poor choices you made. God used even those to make you into the person you are today.

As you look over your list, do you notice a pattern? This is where Romans 8:28 helps us: "We know that all that happens to us is working for our good if we love God and are fitting into his plans" (TLB). This verse can seem empty when we're in the midst of suffering and difficult times, yet it becomes the root and foundation of what keeps us going.

Joseph knew that God was his only hope. God is also *our* only hope. But what makes a man or woman willing to live on that hope? It's a choice—a choice to believe and act in harmony with this belief. It's *The Joseph Road*.

WHAT BRINGS US TO BROKENNESS

Joseph walked the path of brokenness and emerged a whole man. When he had power to destroy, he chose to rescue and save—

both the Egyptians and his family. When he had opportunity for revenge and retribution, he decided to be loving and generous.

Think of the circumstances that typically bring us to a point of brokenness:

Moral Failure

We can relate to David in Psalm 51. Moral failure is never pretty or excusable, but it is forgivable. And it's not the end of your life but the beginning of a new path of righteousness. As Jesus said to the woman caught in adultery, "Go and sin no more."[13] We cannot undo the past, but we can make restitution. Mostly we can walk the path of brokenness before God.

Physical Illness

No one can escape illness. We're human. And in the brokenness of illness, more than in health, we discover who we are.

As I write this, my friend Jerry Armstrong is battling acute leukemia — a virulent, ultimately incurable cancer. When it was discovered, he was told that without treatment, he had eight days to live. Weeks later, after treatment, he was finally able to go home with the disease in remission. He still has a long way to go for full recovery, and he's still battling.

If I ever face such a trial, I hope I'll do half as well as Jerry, whose concern was that his family and the caregivers would see Jesus in the process of his illness. He told his son during this time, "No one knows how he or she will respond in times of crisis."

His son gave this report from Jerry's bedside:

Tuesday Morning 4:15 a.m.

When I came in last evening, Dad was beginning to get tired but was anxious to write a Christmas note to everyone. I told him we could start in the morning when he was rested, but he pointed out that it *was* morning (12:15 a.m.).

As he tried to stay awake to start the note, he began by telling me that *making a difference in people's lives and pointing them to Christ does not take much,* just the will to invest yourself in serving others.

Now, a few hours later, I am rummaging through his Bible, reading the various notes he has made in the margins and on loose pages. On a page dated 12/2/90, titled "My Life Purpose (updated)," he writes:

"To impart my life to others through becoming what God wants me to be as I seek the things above and not the things on earth"—Taken from 1 Thessalonians 2:8 and Colossians 3:1-2."

Family Difficulties

Is the "perfect marriage" a myth? No one has an ideal marriage. All of us experience ups and downs. As sinners, we often hurt those closest to us, especially our spouses.

Conflict, divorce, and remarriage shatter our dreams. Many have divorced, remarried, and then come to a deeper commitment to Christ, wishing they could redo the past. Our children bring us both joy and sorrow. Whether from illness or rebellion, they can turn our parental world upside down as they experience difficult issues. All these are breaking experiences.

Results of Our Sin

"You may be sure that your sin will find you out."[14] Nothing is more sure. Our sin will ultimately be discovered by others or it will work on us from the inside out.

This happens whether our sin is in the form of direct outward disobedience to God's command or consists of inner issues such as pride, arrogance, or covetousness.

Shame from Life Events

Most of us cannot go through life without feeling some measure of shame from many sources. Failure at work or in our family, burn-out, or losing face in some public exposure brings a measure of shame that leads to brokenness. Emotional struggles and depression can undermine our confidence.

The Spiritual Battle

Finally, there's the brokenness that comes from ongoing spiritual battle in the realms of the flesh and the Devil. None of us is exempt in that battle.

Each of these circumstances can lead to the opportunity of being broken before God. Then we have different paths to choose from:

- Rebel and grow bitter.
- Gradually give in, under the nagging and incessant pressure.
- Respond to God with true brokenness.

Joseph is our model for the last choice.

QUESTIONS FOR REFLECTION

1. What would be included on your own list of life events that have defined your life?

2. What's the difference between being *brokenhearted* and being truly *broken* before God?

3. How did Joseph's responses in his trials differ from the responses of his ten brothers in their trials?

4. In relevance to your own life, what are the key events of *The Joseph Road* that you've discerned so far?

If you wish to know what a man is, place him in authority.

—YUGOSLAV PROVERB

Joseph brought his father Jacob in and presented him before Pharaoh. . . . Jacob blessed Pharaoh.

—GENESIS 47:7

CHAPTER 15

SIGNPOST:
Honor Your Elders and Benefactors — Do Your Job Well

HONOR AND RESCUE

When his family moved to Egypt, Joseph was completing his ninth year as prime minister. The famine had lasted two years already. Five tough years were still to come.[1] Only Joseph was absolutely certain about those five years; ordinary Egyptians always had the expectation the famine would end sooner. Each year they hoped, only to be disappointed again.

Meanwhile, Joseph's brothers were still somewhat in shock, not knowing much of their future. It's true Joseph had promised to give them good land in Egypt. They had hope but no guarantees. I compare their situation with that of the pioneers of the early American West who left everything behind, loaded what they could carry into wagons, and struck out for the frontier.

143

BUILT-UP TRUST

Despite his exalted position, Joseph was still a man under authority. He couldn't simply bring his family and give them land. He went to Pharaoh with five of his brothers, and when Pharaoh asked their occupation, the brothers answered as Joseph had instructed them: They were shepherds. For some reason, Egyptians detested shepherds, so Pharaoh was happy to have them locate in their own set-apart area.

Pharaoh so valued and respected Joseph that he told him, "Settle your father and brothers in the best part of the land." He even invited them to be involved in caring for the royal livestock.[2] All this happened because Joseph had been a faithful, loyal, and competent servant of Pharaoh. They'd worked together for nine years, during which this trust was earned and built.

In the world of work, trust and relationships are built over time. They're tested again and again. Then when a favor or something special is needed, the request is almost perfunctory.

I've personally experienced this many times in my Air Force career. I remember once being "dressed down" verbally by a four-star general when I was a two-star general. He was upset because I'd made decisions to eliminate several of his authorized general officer positions in the Air Force Reserves. But I told him the truth about the process and some facts about some of his subordinate commanders and their lack of support. It wasn't a fun conversation.

A few months later, I found out he was to become my new commander. I called him and essentially offered my resignation but suggested I should brief him on my responsibilities. He suggested we meet at a mutual friend's ranch in rural Texas because it was about halfway between where I was staying and where he had his current command headquarters. He planned on flying there in a small Air Force plane.

On the morning of our proposed meeting, fog covered all that part of Texas, restricting flying. I assumed there would be no meeting. When I called him, he said would come by car instead — a three-hour drive instead of a thirty-minute flight. I was impressed. Somehow a mutual respect developed between us, and he kept me in my job. Very likely, he'd checked up on me with my current commander, or he simply knew I would operate with truthfulness and integrity. He never told me for sure, but I know we connected.

RESPECTING AUTHORITY

Joseph also brought his father before Pharaoh. We're told twice that in that meeting, "Jacob blessed Pharaoh."[3] Normally, the greater one blesses the lesser one; here, the wandering foreigner Jacob imparted a blessing on a mighty pagan king. And lest we think this was only a formalized greeting, the same Hebrew word (*barak*) is used later when Jacob blesses Joseph's sons, Ephraim and Manasseh.[4]

What do we make of this encounter?

Remember that earlier, Pharaoh had given Joseph the ultimate authority for rescuing Jacob and his family and bringing them to Egypt. In the same way, secular authorities are used by God to serve His purposes and to bless or curse God-fearing believers. In the New Testament, Christians are instructed to give thanks for secular authorities and to obey them, "that we may live peaceful and quiet lives in all godliness and holiness."[5] Paul puts it more bluntly, telling us that a secular governing official "is God's servant to do you good."[6]

As believers, we should bless and encourage our governmental and business leaders. Part of *The Joseph Road* is to show great respect for authority. This was a consistent theme in Joseph's life as he served under Potiphar, under the chief jailer, and finally under Pharaoh. He was a man under authority, and we should be also.

Living rightly under authority opens the door for the gospel. One of my good friends lived most of his life under the suffocating, oppressive rule of a Communist government in Eastern Europe. He risked much to live for Christ. He was constantly interrogated and watched, protected only by his having earned the Order of Lenin award for his research. In his work, he learned how to conduct himself wisely yet without compromise.

RESCUING PEOPLE, ENRICHING PHARAOH

With Joseph's brothers and father and their families now safely settled in Egypt, Joseph continued his masterful administration over the nation as the famine crisis stretched on, year after year.

It wasn't long before all available money among the people had already been paid to Pharaoh in exchange for grain. Everyone was now broke. Joseph therefore told the people to hand over their livestock in exchange for food. Pharaoh became owner of all the livestock in the country.

Eventually the people came to Joseph and said, "We cannot hide from our lord the fact that since our money is gone and our livestock belongs to you, there is nothing left for our lord except our bodies and our land."[7] Joseph then accepted their land and service as payment. The takeover was complete:

> Joseph bought all the land in Egypt for Pharaoh. The Egyptians, one and all, sold their fields, because the famine was too severe for them. The land became Pharaoh's, and Joseph reduced the people to servitude, from one end of Egypt to the other.[8]

There's no record of the people being forced to do this, but what other options were there? The only ones who kept their lands were the priests because they received food allotment from Pharaoh and never had to buy their food.

There's no specific mention that the land buy-up applied also to Joseph's people in Goshen. If they were exempted, it no doubt gave rise to bitterness on the part of the Egyptians.

Joseph knew when the years of famine were nearing their end. At that time, he gave the Egyptians seed to plant crops, but he made them pledge to give one fifth of their crop to Pharaoh. So the people's money, livestock, land, and freedom had been taken away. One would think they would become angry and bitter over this, even given to mass demonstrations or protests. Not so. Instead they told Joseph, "You have saved our lives. . . . We will be in bondage to Pharaoh."[9]

These actions by Joseph may appear unjust, but they saved millions of lives. No doubt word came in from surrounding countries of the deadly devastation caused by the famine, while the Egyptians survived reasonably well because of Joseph's wisdom.

That wisdom was the result of being faithful to his task. In the God-given interpretation of Pharaoh's dream, Joseph learned of the coming crisis for Egypt as well as its exact timing and the precise instructions for surviving it.[10] So Joseph was not only doing his job but also fulfilling God's clear command.

Every person, great or small, has responsibility to authorities at work or in government. The responsibility may well involve hard decisions of hiring and firing, reducing salaries, punishing lawbreakers, selecting and promoting leaders (while *not* selecting and promoting others), holding people accountable, reprimanding, and myriad other difficult tasks. Joseph, too, made hard decisions, and he did so with God-honoring faithfulness to his responsibilities.

HONORING PARENTS

What do we learn about *The Joseph Road* from this part of the story?

We see the importance of honoring parents. We live in an age of parent bashing, broken families, blame and shame. The culture of honoring parents and elders has given way to a very self-centered view.

No parent is perfect. Every parent is a novice, coming into child-rearing with no experience and few models. With so many divorces in our culture, few homes provide healthy patterns and models, so there are ample gaps in parenting skills in most families. But most parents do the best they can with the training and tools they have, and they deserve honor for that. Few children, even when they become adults, understand the sacrifices, stresses, and efforts made on their behalf by their parents.

"Honor your father and mother—which is the first command-ment with a promise"[11]—that's a New Testament command, but it receives only minor notice today. The vast majority of coun-seling, both Christian and secular, starts first with searching a person's past to explain their present behavior or feelings, and a focus on parental shortcomings is common; this can be legitimate for explanation and understanding but not for blame. Neither the child nor the parent can undo the past. Taking personal respon-sibility is key.

This Joseph did. His home was dysfunctional, yet he chose to honor his father. It was a conscious choice, for he knew that God had orchestrated all of his life.

In my own past, my father essentially abandoned me and my mother. There was no support. When I met him for the first time, at age thirteen, it was with a combination of fear and curiosity. In subsequent years, as he expressed his regret at never supporting me, I felt no bitterness or resentment and I honored both him and my stepfather. And as I began to understand better what my mother had experienced and endured, it caused me to honor her even more.

I've encountered many parents over the last few years who have been cut off from their children or grandchildren for the wrongs they supposedly committed as parents. There's little sense of honor, only blame. Even when resolution occurs, it's often pain-fully slow. When that's the case, something's dreadfully wrong. But God is still at work. He can bring about reconciliation. Being willing to walk through that complex process requires much faith and perseverance.

For some, the situation may never resolve, but we must be committed to keep trying.

SERVE PEOPLE

Another lesson we learn from this part of Joseph's story is our obligation to serve others.

In church, in our community, and at work, God blesses those who sacrificially serve others. Whether as a leader or a follower, a sense of responsibility to look out for the welfare of others is imperative.

Recently in our city, an annual Christmas giveaway was about to be canceled at the last minute due to the serious illness of the sponsor. A local businessman and his wife heard about it and immediately said they would take over. With just days to plan, they mobilized more than one thousand volunteers, delivered hundreds of turkeys, fed three thousand people dinner, and gave away mounds of clothes, hundreds of toys, and more than five hundred bicycles. To accomplish this, they recruited the help of fifteen churches, the United Way, and various city agencies.

This same businessman told me that as they give to the poor, they help people to help themselves and they hold them account-able. One of their remarkable follow-up plans was to allow the people who received help to then give help to others. Hundreds volunteered to help others as they were helped. When you have a heart to serve people, God will open the right doors in your work, neighborhood, or school.

Joseph rescued his family and an entire nation. Perhaps you can rescue your neighborhood. This doesn't mean offering food and assistance in exchange for being given an opportunity to pres-ent the gospel. The gospel is lived out by your actions, your love, and your compassion. When people ask, "Why are you doing this?" then you can speak.

As I write this today, I've just conducted the funeral of a nine-month-old baby born in difficult circumstances and missing part of his little heart. The parents were teenagers, now estranged. I felt inadequate to conduct the funeral, yet this was where Mary and I knew we needed to be and to serve.

The teenage friends of this couple flocked to the graveside. Afterward, the brother of the teen father came up and thanked me not just for the service but also for visiting him in the hospital months earlier, after he'd been nearly fatally stabbed. I wish I could say this kind of service was a pattern of my life, but in reality, it was a one-time event.

Maybe God has some one-time events in store for you. Serve others and you'll never regret it.

QUESTIONS FOR REFLECTION

1. How can you best honor your parents right now?
2. How can you best serve other people in your world?
3. Do you think Joseph acted unjustly in accumulating all the land for Pharaoh?
4. To whom was Joseph accountable? How was he able to balance serving God and his job?
5. How would you have responded if your brothers had treated you as Joseph's brothers treated him?

It is not how much we have, but how much we enjoy,
that makes happiness.
— CHARLES HADDON SPURGEON

Your father's blessings are greater
than the blessings of the ancient mountains,
than the bounty of the age-old hills.
Let all these rest on the head of Joseph,
on the brow of the prince among his brothers.
— GENESIS 49:26

CHAPTER **16**

SIGNPOST:
Bless the People You Love

BLESSING

I f you're among nursing home residents, it takes only a few moments to become intimately aware of the carnage of age. Their infirmities of body and mind are only too obvious, reminding us that one day we'll be there too. Their wisdom and accomplishments live in the dustbin of time, memories that only they possess. Yet they're still wise and gifted, and they're real people with real needs.

As a society, we pay little attention to older people. When we do pay attention, it's most often because they're our parents or grandparents. Depending on our history with them, we desperately want their blessing and acceptance.

Blessing becomes a key theme as the story of Joseph begins drawing to a close in the book of Genesis. In Egypt, the descendants of Joseph's father, Jacob, were on their way to rapid expansion:

> The Israelites settled in Egypt in the region of Goshen. They acquired property there and were fruitful and increased greatly in number.[1]

Jacob himself lived in Egypt for seventeen years until "the time drew near" for him to die. He took the initiative to call Joseph into his presence and made a strange request to his powerful son:

> If I have found favor in your eyes, put your hand under my thigh [an ancient way to demonstrate loyalty to a promise] and promise that you will show me kindness and faithfulness. Do not bury me in Egypt, but when I rest with my fathers, carry me out of Egypt and bury me where they are buried.[2]

Joseph agreed to this solemn promise.

In response, his father "bowed his head in submission and gratitude from his bed."[3]

Joseph was again honoring his father and realized his own responsibility for the family.

As our parents get older, we as their children care for them and honor them. It's one of the greatest privileges of our lives to serve our parents in this manner. At the same time, we desperately want their blessing—for ourselves and our children. This is part of *The Joseph Road*. Honor and blessing are intimately connected.

IMPARTING A BLESSING

At this point in Genesis, the focus shifts to the blessings Jacob will impart to his sons and grandsons.

The old patriarch had become bedridden and his "eyes were failing because of old age, and he could hardly see."[4] But in the pattern of ancient times, he still had great power and influence in the family. Inheritance and blessings were at the complete option of the patriarch or elder, whose decisions were crucial to the future of the clan.

Jacob would give two kinds of blessing: the first was a blessing of priority and preeminence; the second was a mix of blessing and prophecy.

Joseph learned that his father was ill and seemed to be dying. Joseph went to him, taking also his two sons, Ephraim and Manasseh, who by that time were young men. He wanted his father to bless them. Before proceeding with that blessing, the dying man went far beyond blessing. Jacob restated God's promise to him about establishing and prospering a nation from his descendants:

Jacob said to Joseph, "The Strong God appeared to me at Luz in the land of Canaan and blessed me. He said, 'I'm going to make you prosperous and numerous, turn you into a congregation of tribes; and I'll turn this land over to your children coming after you as a permanent inheritance.'"[5]

Then he announced a decision that must have astonished Joseph:

I'm adopting your two sons who were born to you here in Egypt before I joined you; they have equal status with Reuben and Simeon. But any children born after them are yours; they will come after their brothers in matters of inheritance. I want it this way because, as I was returning from Paddan, your mother Rachel, to my deep sorrow, died as we were on our way through Canaan when we were only a short distance from Ephrath, now called Bethlehem.[6]

Jacob asked his grandsons Ephraim and Manasseh to step near so he could bless them. He embraced and kissed the young men.

Joseph then honored his father again by bowing his face to the ground. Jacob blessed his two grandsons (although, to Joseph's surprise, he gave his greater, "right-hand" blessing not to Joseph's firstborn, Manasseh, but to the younger son, Ephraim).

Jacob also "blessed Joseph" at this time and expressed a blessing that covered both of Joseph's sons:

> May the God before whom my fathers
>   Abraham and Isaac walked,
> the God who has been my shepherd
>   all my life to this day,
> the Angel who has delivered me from all harm
>   — may he bless these boys.
> May they be called by my name
>   and the names of my fathers Abraham and Isaac,
> and may they increase greatly
>   upon the earth.[7]

Jacob then spoke words to Joseph indicating his faith in God's higher plan for his descendants: "I am about to die, but *God will be with you and take you back to the land of your fathers*"[8] In Hebrew, the "you" in these verses is plural, pointing not to Joseph but to all the future nation of Israel.

Soon Jacob called together his twelve sons and declared prophecies concerning each. When he spoke of Joseph, his words were richly positive while also clearly indicating that Jacob knew what his other sons had done to Joseph. In fact, in his prophetic words regarding all twelve of his sons, a specific conferral of blessing is included only in his words to Joseph:

> Joseph is a fruitful vine. . . .
> With bitterness archers attacked him;
>   they shot at him with hostility.
> But his bow remained steady,
>   his strong arm stayed limber,
> because of the hand of the Mighty One of Jacob,
>   because of the Shepherd, the Rock of Israel,
> because of your father's God, who helps you,
>   because of the Almighty, who blesses you
> with blessings of the heavens above,
>   blessings of the deep that lies below,
>   blessings of the breast and womb.
> Your father's blessings are greater
>   than the ancient mountains,
>   than the bounty of the age-old hills.
> Let all these rest on the head of Joseph,
>   on the brow of the *prince among his brothers*.[9]

HOW WE BLESS

In *The Joseph Road*, where does blessing fit? We're not Jacob, one of the heroes of Israel, the father of a nation. Nor are we Joseph, a powerful political personage. We're ordinary men and women with complicated families and relationships. Many of us have already passed up prime opportunities to bless our children, grandchildren, and parents. We can start only where we are. We cannot rewind the tape, but we can repair some of the past.

Gary Smalley and John Trent's insightful book *The Blessing* gives extensive ideas on giving blessings. They write,

> Gaining or missing out on parental approval has a tremendous effect on us, even if it has been years since we have had any regular contact with them. In fact, what happens in our relationship with our parents can greatly affect all our present and future relationships.[10]

The effect of giving or receiving blessing is tremendous. It is biblical and imperative.

OUR SPOKEN WORDS

What we say and how we say it impacts children all their lives. In fact, it profoundly affects everyone we speak with. Learn to speak kind and encouraging words. Guard your criticism. Speak positive things.

I'm not advocating empty words that our children will see as insincere. It won't work to tell them they're the best player on the soccer team when they know they're not. Speak truth. Look for the good things they do.

Earlier I referred to my former history teacher who lived to be 107 years old. I still remember a comment he made about me in class. When I sat down after finishing an oral report on a Civil War battle, he said, "Now, that's the way a report ought to be given!" I lived for years on that comment. It meant so much because most of my classmates were from the "right side of town," while I was not. His spoken praise told me I could compete with those from better backgrounds. Obviously, I've never forgotten it.

On the opposite side, I remember bringing home a "straight A" report card. My stepfather, who wasn't an effusive person, acknowledged it, but there was little comment. Eventually I came to understand that this was part of his personality. He was a kind man who labored hard to support our family. In no way do I resent or blame him. But I would have loved to hear from him an occasional "Wow, good job!"

Blessing can also come through written words. Write notes of commendation and encouragement to your children and grandchildren. Birthday cards are one way to do this, but they're an expected expression. Do it at random and special times: after sports events, plays, school functions, or school achievements. Make a deliberate effort at this especially when you don't live near them. E-mail is a weak substitute for a written note, although it can be good for "quick kudos" and "thinking of you" notes. Learn to text message the younger ones. They live by it daily.

Blessing comes particularly through words of praise. Praising others is an art. It's more than saying, "Well done." Praise cannot be empty. Be specific and genuine: "That was a really a great move you made in the second period of the wrestling match. What was it?" "I really liked the way you treated that girl. She doesn't have many friends, and you went out of your way to talk to her."

Don't do as I did with one of my teenage daughters. She once asked what I thought of her skirt, which I thought was too short. Without thinking, I said, "I think I would burn it." She was crushed. My words were thoughtless and hurtful, and she has never let me forget it, although now it's a family joke.

The most significant thing we can do to bless our family is to pray regularly for them, specifically and intensely. Let them know the specific things you're praying. "We always thank God for all of you, mentioning you in our prayers."[11]

What should we pray? Paul's example offers a trustworthy outline:

> We have not stopped praying for you and asking God to fill you with knowledge of his will through all spiritual wisdom and understanding . . . that you may live lives worthy of the Lord and may please him in every way: bearing fruit in every good work, growing in the knowledge of God, being strengthened with all power according to his glorious might so that you may have great endurance and patience.[12]

What more could we want?

OUR LEGACY

What Jacob gave his sons—especially Joseph—was a priceless legacy. What legacy will you leave to those you love?

We most often think of legacy in terms of physical and legal inheritance. But it's much broader, involving inheritance and possessions, memories, spiritual matters, and your presence.

Here are some ideas to consider that hopefully will seed your thinking for your particular situation.

Inheritance and Possessions

First, you must have a will. Without it, you set your family up for conflict and resentment. If you possess significant assets, you need help from professional planners. There are many excellent resources to help you put together a will. One is Crown Ministries (www.crown.org), which offers a free will-planning kit.

A large inheritance rarely serves the heirs well. Consider the following ideas:

- Give most away before you die.
- Give modest amounts, with no restrictions, to your heirs.
- Provide encouragement for the inheritance to be used for the values you have. (The movie and book *The Ultimate Gift*[13] is an excellent stimulus to doing this.)
- Specify the most important items to be given to each heir.
- Be equitable so as not to engender conflict.
- Skip a generation to grandchildren, especially for education and ministry development.
- Let your values guide how the money is used. Consider

some kind of trust that encourages education, mission trips, purchasing a first home, or paying for major medical expenses.

You don't have to be wealthy to do this. Just your home can be a major part of your estate.

Have a realistic grasp of what you really have in the way of possessions. Most of the things people own have insignificant monetary value — clothes, furniture, dishes, and so on. (For Mary and me, almost everything in our house would barely make a good garage sale.) The items of real value are those that connect us with other family members. Some items are of great sentimental value, such as awards, degree certificates, military uniforms, photographs, journals, letters, your generational history, your personal Bibles and favorite books.

Above all, compose a written letter to as many of your heirs as you can. Remember, it's *you* they value, not your things.

Memories

We have close friends, Dr. Stan and Lois Newell, whose favorite sayings is "Let's make a memory." Great advice! What you'll give to your children and grandchildren are items that bring back memories.

We may not know for sure what will give your loved ones a good memory. Certainly photos and videos are key. Your personal history will become more precious to them as time goes on. Make a video or recording of your personal history: your special journey, your parents and grandparents, where you grew up, why you did many of the things you did, your work, your thinking about them when they were small, your struggles, where you lived, and much more.

You would be surprised how little your children and grand-children really know about you. Should you doubt this, think how much you really know of the true inner lives of your own parents and grandparents.

One of my valued possessions is a journal my great-grand-father kept as he traveled back to Norway and reflected on the spiritual conditions he saw.

In your video or recording, you could even preach. If your loved ones don't now share your spiritual values, your words may later be the key to their lives. If there has been conflict and trouble, leave a message of hope.

A Spiritual Heritage

So many people I talk with tell of their spiritual journal having been influenced by godly grandparents and parents.

Let your children and grandchildren know what you believe. Be real in the telling of your own spiritual struggles. Share with them the mistakes you've made. After all, everyone makes mistakes. J. M. Barrie, the Scottish author and dramatist and creator of *Peter Pan*, wisely commented, "The life of every man is a diary in which he means to write one story and writes another; his humblest hour is when he compares the volume as it is with what he hoped to make it."[14]

Your Presence

Nothing is a substitute for being there with your children and grandchildren. Hugs and kisses don't go easily by mail. Presence speaks loudly.

One of the disappointments of my early life is that I don't recall my parents coming to any of my athletic or school events. My memory may be faulty, but that's what I recall.

For your children and grandchildren, make the effort to be there at key events, athletic competitions, school award presentations, birthdays, weddings, and graduations. When you live far away, plan those special trips. Make it a priority.

Seven of our eleven grandchildren live in our city. Their activities go on our calendar first. They don't say much about our presence, but they see us. At sports events, we get their sweaty hugs, yell for them, commend them, and encourage them. For the four grandchildren who live at a distance, it's more difficult. Travel, phone calls, and pictures are part of our plan. In this way, we bless them with something that's never forgotten: our presence.

Alex Haley once said, "Nobody can do for little children what grandparents do. Grandparents sort of sprinkle stardust over the lives of little children."[15]

UNBLESSING

What are the consequences of not passing on a blessing—or worse, of purposely withholding or withdrawing our blessing?

In *What's So Amazing About Grace?* Philip Yancey cites a sad account of a lack of blessing in the life of the famous author Ernest Hemingway:

> Hemingway knew about the ungrace of families. His devout parents—Hemingway's grandparents had attended evangelical Wheaton College—detested Hemingway's

libertine life, and after a time his mother refused to allow him in her presence. One year for his birthday, she mailed him a cake along with the gun his father had used to kill himself. Another year she wrote him a letter explaining that a mother's life is like a bank. "Every child that is born to her enters the world with a large and prosperous bank account, seemingly inexhaustible." The child, she continued, makes withdrawals but no deposits during all its early years. Later, when the child grows up, it is his responsibility to replenish the supply he has drawn down. Hemingway's mother then proceeded to spell out all the specific ways in which Ernest should be making "deposits to keep the account in good standing": flowers, fruit or candy, a surreptitious paying of Mother's bills, and above all a determination to stop "neglecting your duties to God and your Saviour, Jesus Christ." Hemingway never got over his hatred for his mother or for her Savior. [Hemingway shot himself on July 2, 1961.[16]

One final thought: Most of the blessings in the Bible are by men to other young men. Is there any material difference in blessing given or received by women? No such difference has biblical foundation.

Authority often rests with the man, the patriarch of a family. Many children struggle when they don't have their father's involvement and blessing. To counter this, the most revered figures in many families are women: mothers and grandmothers. Women more naturally bless and encourage. Men more naturally correct and critique.

In a day of broken marriages, the intact family is a rarity, so often the blessing is left to solitary attempts by an estranged or distant mother or father. This is reality. In such circumstances, it's even more vital for moms and dads, grandmothers and grandfathers, to step in and actually bless children and young adults.

Don't wait until it's too late. Start now.

QUESTIONS FOR REFLECTION

1. What kinds of blessings have you received in your life?
2. Describe some ways you've attempted to bless family members and others.
3. What lessons do you see from Joseph's response to his father? How fair was Jacob in his blessings and prophecies?
4. Describe some changes you can make in the next year to bless your children and grandchildren.

Cowards are cruel, but the brave love mercy and delight to save.

—JOHN GAY

Am I in the place of God?

—GENESIS 50:19

CHAPTER 17

SIGNPOST:
Always Give Grace

ACTING WITH GRACE

When Jacob died, panic set in for Joseph's brothers. All the cards were now on the table. From Jacob's parting words of prophecy and blessing, they knew the inheritance that each brother would receive. They knew that preeminence had been given to Joseph—he was clearly in charge.

As for Joseph, he was heartbroken over his father's death. As Jacob breathed his last breath, "Joseph threw himself upon his father and wept over him and kissed him."[1]

All the family joined in the formal mourning. In the custom of Egypt—new to Jacob's family—they embalmed Jacob's body. In accordance with his wishes, the entire family, with Pharaoh's permission, went to Canaan to bury him. All the pomp and pageantry of a royal Egyptian funeral was on display, with key leaders of Egypt joining the family to accompany the body to Canaan. Jacob was buried near the graves of his wives, Rachel and Leah.

Now that all the formal mourning was completed, the brothers gathered with fear and trepidation:

> When Joseph's brothers saw that their father was dead, they said, "What if Joseph holds a grudge against us and pays us back for all the wrongs we did to him?"[2]

Once again, the brothers' true colors showed. They had a guilty conscience. They knew they'd sinned against God, against Jacob, and against Joseph. When they spoke of "all the wrongs we did to him," they knew each wrong in great detail. Night and day they had replayed the evil and kept it hidden from their father. How many meals had they had together at home when Jacob spoke of his lost son and they had to relive the lies they'd told him?

THE DIFFICULTY OF A CLEAR CONSCIENCE

Sin is like that. It constantly confronts us. The Holy Spirit convicts and causes us to wrestle with whether we'll confess and repent.

One of our overarching goals must be to pursue a clean and clear conscience. Paul, who had the murder of believers on his conscience, expressed it this way: "I strive always to keep my conscience clear before God and man."[3] The words *strive* and *always* paint a picture of how difficult it is to maintain a clear conscience.

Paul, with his background and brilliance, always battled his part in the persecution of believers and his natural sinful tendencies. As a leader, he had to work at being direct, forthright, and truthful in all his actions.

Today we have the Holy Spirit as well as God's Scriptures to help us deal with a guilty conscience. The book of Hebrews, written to the descendants of Israel, describes how to maintain a clear conscience. Referring to the inability of the law and good works to cleanse us from sin, Hebrews describes Jesus Christ as our Great High Priest who Himself became a sacrifice for us: "How much more, then, will the blood of Christ, who through the eternal Spirit offered himself unblemished to God, cleanse our consciences from acts that lead to death, so that we may serve the living God!"[4]

In this age of grace, the only way to a clear conscience is through Jesus Christ, whose life and ministry was foreshadowed in many ways in the life of Joseph.

THE UNIMAGINABLE RESPONSE

Joseph's brothers were deeply troubled. With their father's presence and influence now gone forever, how would Joseph treat them? If they were in his sandals, they knew *they* would have sought revenge, so they assumed Joseph would do the same. With that assumption, they conspired together and sent Joseph what was apparently another set of lies while daring to speak of themselves as God's servants:

> They sent word to Joseph, saying, "Your father left these instructions before he died: 'This is what you are to say to Joseph: I ask you to forgive your brothers the sins and the wrongs they committed in treating you so badly.' Now

please forgive the sins of the servants of the God of your
father."[5]

What a sad commentary on these men who were the found-
ers of the tribes of Israel. It seemed they had learned so little of
Joseph's character or of how Joseph thought and functioned. After
all, if he'd wanted, he could have easily taken revenge long before.
But just as his brothers showed their true colors, so also Joseph
showed his: "When their message came to him, Joseph wept."[6]

Joseph surely must have known they were lying about the
supposed message from their father. His human response could
easily have been anger and retaliation. Instead, he broke down
and cried. I think he cried because he realized how little his brothers had learned and changed and how little they understood
both about him and about God's care for them. After sending
the request to Joseph, their anxieties made them desperate: "His
brothers then came and threw themselves down before him. 'We
are your slaves,' they said."[7]

Yet again the image from Joseph's dreams is acted out in reality, as he must have recalled once more. Joseph's answer is remarkable: "Don't be afraid. Am I in the place of God? You intended
to harm me, but God intended it for good to accomplish what is
now being done, the saving of many lives."[8]

Joseph acknowledged the sovereign plan of God for himself
and for all of them. He didn't let them off the hook, clearly stating
that they had indeed intended to harm him. Yet that very situation was something God intended for good. Why? To accomplish
His purposes.

Joseph acted with grace and kindness, and the brothers

could hardly believe it. They couldn't imagine such a response, as it would have been the last thing they themselves would think to do.

A PATH OF GRACE

The Joseph Road is a path of grace.

The picture of grace in *The Joseph Road* is that of grace given and grace received. When Joseph had the power to crush his brothers, he gave them grace instead. They didn't deserve it, and they hadn't earned it. He was an instrument of grace on God's behalf for them.

We must choose to give grace rather than revenge or retribution. How can you give grace?

One way is to guard your speech. Speak with grace and kindness. "Let your conversation be always full of grace, seasoned with salt, so that you may know how to answer everyone."[9] As followers of Jesus, we show grace by how we speak: "Do not let any unwholesome talk come out of your mouths, only what is helpful for building others up according to their needs, that it may benefit those who listen."[10]

Grace is expressed by gracious words, while harsh words destroy people, friendships, and marriages.

A word out of your mouth may seem of no account, but it can accomplish nearly anything—or destroy it! . . . A careless or wrongly placed word out of your mouth can do that. By our speech we can ruin the world, turn harmony to chaos, throw mud on a reputation, send the whole world up in smoke and go up in smoke with it, smoke right from the pit of hell.[11]

To walk *The Joseph Road*, we must learn to speak and act with grace. But we can't do this on our own. We just aren't built that way. We can show grace only when we've *received* grace.

UNEARNED

Grace is a gift. It cannot be earned. Joseph's brothers did absolutely nothing to earn what Joseph gave them: freedom and protection.

One of the most difficult truths to grasp about being a believer and follower of Jesus centers in the understanding of grace. God gave a special promise to Joseph's great-grandfather, Abraham, and this was long before the Law of Moses was given. Abraham obeyed God by going to Canaan, where God told him to go:

> That famous promise God gave Abraham—that he and his children would possess the earth—was not given because of something Abraham did or would do. It was based on God's decision to put everything together for him, which Abraham then entered when he believed. If those who get what God gives them only get it by doing everything they are told to do and filling out all the right forms properly signed, that eliminates personal trust completely and turns the promise into an ironclad *contract*! That's not a holy promise; that's a business deal. A contract drawn up by a hard-nosed lawyer and with plenty of fine print only makes sure that you will never be

able to collect. But if there is no contract in the first place, simply a *promise*—and God's promise at that—you can't break it.[12]

Paul states the truth of grace profoundly in these words:

God, who is rich in mercy, made us alive with Christ even when we were dead in transgressions. . . . For it is by grace you have been saved, though faith—and this not from yourselves, it is the gift of God—not by works, so that no one can boast.[13]

Joseph's brothers couldn't strut around proclaiming what good guys they were or how they'd earned Joseph's trust and protection. They were rotten scoundrels, yet Joseph gave them grace.

It's the same with our salvation. We simply accept the grace by placing our faith in Jesus. No contract; just a promise.

This is *The Joseph Road*, a path of grace.

A PATH OF FORGIVENESS

The Joseph Road is also a path of forgiveness.

In grace, forgiveness permeates to the core of our wrongdoing. Grace isn't cheap; it's costly. Joseph's forgiveness of his brothers was based not on their performance or even their outward repentance (though they asked him to forgive) but on his view of God. It is God who forgives. In the Old Testament, forgiveness required sacrifice, but sacrifices don't forgive a person—God chooses to do that.

In the New Testament, Jesus forgave those who wronged Him: "Father, forgive them, for they do not know what they are doing."[14] When we are wronged, we're told to do the same with each other: "Bear with each other and forgive whatever grievances you may have against one other. *Forgive as the Lord forgave you.*"[15]

The Joseph Road means receiving forgiveness from God and giving forgiveness to others.

A PATH OF SUBMISSION TO GOD'S SOVEREIGNTY

The Joseph Road is also a path of submission to the sovereign plan of God.

We may think Joseph's attitude of grace and forgiveness was magnanimous beyond imagination. But it was also the inevitable consequence of his core belief in the loving sovereignty of God in his life and his submission to God's grand plan. Joseph didn't understand this when he endured all the injustices, nor even when he rose to power. But when his brothers came to him for grain, he finally saw it: "God sent me ahead of you to preserve you. . . . You intended to harm me, but God intended it for good."[16] Joseph saw his higher authority—God—and he submitted to that authority.

Such submission is hard. When our life crashes in at work, in our family, or with our health, we puzzle over the "Why?"

I searched desperately for God's plan when our son was murdered. Reflecting later, I wrote these words: "There is more to life than being alive. There is an eternal life with God that supersedes all the goals of humanity."

Now I see some of God's purposes—certainly not all, but some. He crushed my pride and ego. He sent me back to the basics of my beliefs about God. He drove me to the Scriptures. He opened doors to other peoples' lives in a profound way. He put my achievements where they belonged: in the trash bin. He drove me to submit to His sovereign plan.

Romans 8:28 can come across as a trite saying, but it rings true during the difficulties of life: "We *know* that in *all* things God works for the good of those who love him, who have been called *according to his purpose*."

We cannot go through life wondering if God knows what He's doing. We endure and submit because we trust a loving God to work in us and on our behalf.

The Joseph Road wraps grace, forgiveness, and submission in one package. When we open that package, we'll experience an incredible joy and peace. But if we refuse this gift, we won't experience all that God has for us. We cannot change the events, but we can alter our response.

QUESTIONS FOR REFLECTION

1. Why did Joseph respond as he did?
2. Why is grace sometimes so difficult to receive?
3. Compare the grace that gives us salvation with the grace we need in living out the life of a believer. What's the difference?
4. What are some events in your life that have driven you to God? How could you have responded better? What further response is needed from you now?
5. How do you most often extend grace to others?

Trust the past to God's mercy, the present to God's love, and the future to God's providence.

— AUGUSTINE

I am about to die. But God will surely come to your aid and take you up out of this land to the land he promised on oath to Abraham, Isaac and Jacob.

— GENESIS 50:24

CHAPTER 18 →

SIGNPOST:
Prepare for the Last Act

FAITHFUL TO THE END

n a sports contest, no matter how well the game is played, people usually remember only the final result. How we finish reflects how we've lived.

For *The Joseph Road*, the finish—the culmination—is a commitment to the future, preceded by grace given and grace received.

Joseph gave grace to his brothers during his remaining fifty or sixty years. He lived to see his great-great-grandchildren. Finally, when he knew he was about to die, he called his family together and said to his brothers, "I am about to die. But God will surely come to your aid and take you up out of this land to the land he promised on oath to Abraham, Isaac and Jacob."[1]

Then he made them take an unusual oath: "You must carry

my bones up from this place."[2]

Then he died, was embalmed, and was placed in a coffin.

Why did Joseph give that request? And what actually happened?

More than three hundred years after Joseph's request, when the Israelites under Moses finally left Egypt, that request wasn't forgotten:

> Moses took the bones of Joseph with him because Joseph had made the sons of Israel swear an oath. He had said, "God will surely come to your aid, and then you must carry my bones up with you from this place."[3]

After leaving Egypt, the Israelites then carried Joseph's bones for more than forty years of wandering, until the time of Joshua's death. And then:

> Joseph's bones, which the Israelites had brought up from Egypt, were buried at Shechem. . . . This became the inheritance of Joseph's descendants.[4]

In Hebrews 11, a roll call of spiritual heroes, Joseph's final act receives special notice:

> By faith Joseph, when his end was near, spoke about the exodus of the Israelites from Egypt and *gave instructions about his bones.*[5]

Obviously this was a big deal. Why?

- It was a constant reminder of *hope*.
- It was a profound act of *faith* by Joseph.
- It was a symbol of his *legacy*.

NEEDING HOPE

During four centuries of slavery in Egypt, after another Pharaoh arose "who did not know about Joseph,"[6] the Israelites suffered greatly. They had to live on hope, for they had nothing else.

Everyone needs hope. Without hope, we die. We give up. "Hope deferred makes the heart sick."[7]

People vest themselves in two kinds of hope: temporal and eternal.

If our hope is temporal — based on happiness, success, security, and material possessions — it won't last. Many of us will spend our last days in a small room with the remnants of everything we've accumulated in life stored in boxes, given to Goodwill, or distributed to our children. Little remains of our accumulations. Cars, clothing, and houses will be just memories.

We know our lives here are temporary, yet most of us give ourselves to temporal hope. All the success and pop psychology books teach and glorify this kind of hope: Get *more*, and be happy. Make more money and buy more things. Gain position and power for worldly acclaim. Buy a bigger house, a more prestigious car, and a vacation home to feel better about life. All these are temporal. These things in themselves are fine, but not if they're the source of our hope.

What's the source of *your* hope? You can identify it by simply asking yourself, *What regularly occupies my mind? What is my focus and delight?*

Under the reign of grace, our hope should be governed by Christ and His purposes: "Since, then, you have been raised with Christ, set your hearts on things above, where Christ is seated at the right hand of God."[8]

What does it mean to have eternal hope? In the Old Testament, David explained it this way: "But now, Lord, what do I look for? My hope is in you."[9] Our hope in this life is to give ourselves to what will last for eternity: people, God's Word, and a life that reflects Christ. When circumstances become difficult, when our health breaks down or our marriage or family breaks apart, then hope in temporal things gives no comfort. Our hope in Christ is then our only true hope:

> We have peace with God through our Lord Jesus Christ, through whom we have gained access by faith into this grace in which we now stand. And we rejoice in the hope of the glory of God. Not only so, but we also rejoice in our sufferings, because we know that suffering produces perseverance; perseverance, character; and character, hope. And hope does not disappoint us, because God has poured out his love into our hearts by the Holy Spirit, whom he has given us.[10]

Observe the connection of grace, suffering, and hope. Joseph suffered, received and gave grace, and then caused his bones to be a constant reminder of the hope of God's deliverance.

We place our hope in God by first trusting in His Son, Jesus, for our eternal salvation—by grace through faith. Then we govern our lives by that hope. "We have this hope as an anchor for the soul, firm and secure," says the writer of Hebrews, who goes on to describe how this security came through our great high priest, Jesus.[11] And Peter tells us, "Set your hope fully on the grace to be given you when Jesus Christ is revealed."[12]

FAITH AND LEGACY

As I've said, giving instruction about his bones was a profound act of faith on Joseph's part. He'd faithfully worshipped and served the God of his fathers; now he pointed others to faith in God's future deliverance.

His bones were also a symbol of his legacy to the tribes of Israel, the sons of Jacob. Through Joseph, they'd been delivered from famine and death. They would, by the presence of his bones, always be reminded of that deliverance.

What legacy should we most want to leave with our children and grandchildren? Not a legacy of money and property but, as we discussed earlier, a legacy of faith in the living God.

I mentioned earlier my friend Jerry Armstrong and his battle with acute leukemia. He continues to work toward full recovery, but as a result of the battle he's been through, the lives of all his family will never be the same.

Upon entering the hospital, he'd written these words:

Dear God, use me as Your servant to impact lives. Use me to build the faith of my children and grandchildren. . . .

When we think of calamity personally, we generally think of ourselves—what we need, what we want, what we would change. God still has a plan for my life, a plan with a future and a hope. One day, two weeks, ten years—it's a great plan. If my trial impacts but one life, that will be precious.

Jerry also shared a bit of humor:

Is it really true that my illness is "a cute leukemia"? There is nothing cute about it.

In these words I see faith, hope, and legacy in a way that health and success rarely show.

That's why Joseph's last words are so important.

What would your last words be? What will mine be?

Two months ago, while traveling, I was staying in a hotel. Late that night, I began feeling ill. It came over me so quickly that I was about to call 911. I told Mary, "Something's happening to me!" For one of the few times in my life, I envisioned my own imminent death. I'm chagrined to say I felt anxiety and fear.

It turned out to be sudden twenty-four-hour flu. But for the next several weeks, I contemplated my life through a new lens—that of the brevity of my own life and its meaning. I decided (again) that I wanted to finish walking *The Joseph Road* well.

JOSEPH AND JESUS

As this book nears its end, it's good to focus on the highest and most exalted perspective we can have of Joseph: as a picture of Jesus. Many authors and teachers have studied the parallels; one author listed fifty-eight of them.

Consider just a few of them:

Jesus was the beloved son of his Father, God.
> *Joseph was the favorite son of Jacob.*

Jesus was unjustly tried and condemned.
> *Joseph was unjustly treated by his brothers and unjustly convicted and jailed in Egypt.*

Jesus was sold for thirty pieces of silver.
> *Joseph was sold for twenty pieces of silver.*

Jesus suffered on the cross.
> *Joseph suffered as a slave and in prison.*

Jesus was later crowned with glory and honor.
> *Joseph was later made prime minister of Egypt.*

Jesus rescued His people — Israel and the Gentiles — from their sin.
> *Joseph rescued his family and the Egyptians from famine.*

Jesus became Savior to the Gentiles.
> *Joseph was given a Gentile wife and saved the pagan nation of Egypt.*

Jesus was the ultimate Savior with a prophetic view of a final deliverance in the last days.

Joseph saved his people and prophesied the future deliverance from Egypt to the promised land.

Jesus served God's ultimate purpose for the salvation of mankind.

Joseph was God's instrument to save Israel from extinction. God meant it for good.

And there are many more comparisons.

Joseph's life fits well the Christ-centeredness of all the Scriptures: The Old Testament looks forward to Christ; the Gospels reveal Christ; the remaining New Testament books teach us how to know and follow Christ; the book of Revelation sees Christ's future kingdom.

CHOOSE THE JOSEPH ROAD

The Joseph Road lays out a pattern for believers to navigate through life with all its twists and turns. It's filled with choices we must make to keep on that path of blessing.

Make choices that leave no regret. Make choices that lead to a life well lived. As Apollo astronaut Walter Cunningham said, "Don't be one of those souls who says, 'If only I had my life to live over.' Life your life in such a way that once is enough."

QUESTIONS FOR REFLECTION

1. What was Joseph's legacy?
2. What was the significance of Joseph's command about his bones?
3. How can you leave a legacy? And to whom will you leave it?
4. How do hope and faith practically impact your life?
5. What's the significance of the parallels between Jesus and Joseph? What other parallels have you seen?
6. What's the "bottom line" of *The Joseph Road* for you?

A POEM

So few feel what I feel
So few understand
But find that one who does
And you will find a friend
Life struggles to begin
It stumbles to learn and think
Life grows with hope in youth
Trying to find its way
Life soars with success
Thinking well of its gifts
Life sinks as hope crumbles
Weakening in the grim reality
Life is reborn in hope
As new growth springs up
    out of the ashes of suffering
    out of the soil of brokenness
        J. W.

NOTES

CHAPTER 1: I Had a Dream
1. (Genesis 37:6-7).
2. (1 Kings 19:12, NKJV).
3. (Isaiah 30:21).
4. (Proverbs 29:18, MSG).

CHAPTER 2: Shattered Dreams
1. (Genesis 37:18).
2. (37:31-32).
3. (37:33-35).
4. (42:21).
5. (42:22).
6. (Romans 8:28).
7. (Job 30:20, NASB).
8. (Psalm 34:17-18).
9. (Genesis 50:20).

CHAPTER 3: The Source of Success
1. (Genesis 39:1).
2. (39:2-4, emphasis added).
3. (Luke 16:10).
4. (Genesis 39:3).

CHAPTER 4: Doing Right, but Getting Crushed
1. (Genesis 39:6).
2. (39:8-9).

3. (Job 23:10).
4. (Genesis 39:11).
5. (39:12).
6. (39:14-15).
7. (1 Corinthians 10:13).

CHAPTER 5: Up from the Ashes
1. (see Genesis 32:22-32).
2. (see 22:1-14).
3. (Mark 7:37).
4. (Genesis 39:22-23).
5. (see Acts 10:38).
6. (Matthew 6:34).
7. (Ecclesiastes 9:10).

CHAPTER 6: Faithfulness Brings Favor
1. (Genesis 41:14).
2. (see Genesis 39:3-4).
3. (see 39:21).
4. (39:4).
5. (39:22).
6. (39:6).
7. (39:23).
8. (39:3).
9. (39:23).
10. (39:22).
11. (Matthew 28:20).
12. (Colossians 3:23, NASB).
13. (Hebrews 11:35-38).
14. (Proverbs 3:5-6, NKJV).

CHAPTER 7: Building Other People's Dreams
1. (Genesis 40:6).
2. (40:11).
3. (40:13).

4. (40:17).
5. (40:19).
6. (see 40:14-15).
7. (40:23).
8. (Matthew 22:39).

CHAPTER 8: A Twist of Fate
1. (Genesis 41:14).
2. (41:2-6).
3. (41:8).
4 (41:16).
5. (41:16).
6. (41:25).
7. (41:28-30).
8. (see 41:33-36).
9. (Proverbs 16:9).
10. (Proverbs 16:3).
11. (1 Corinthians 4:7).

CHAPTER 9: Seizing the Opportunity
1. (Ecclesiastes 7:14).
2. (Genesis 41:37).
3. (41:38).
4. (41:41,43).

CHAPTER 10: Pressing On
1. (Genesis 41:46-49).
2. (41:52).
3. (41:52).
4. (Job 23:10).
5. (Proverbs 6:6-11, MSG).

CHAPTER 11: When Disaster Strikes, Testing Begins
1. (1 Peter 4:12).

CHAPTER **12: The Game Begins**
1. (Genesis 41:57).
2. (Genesis 42:1).
3. (42:2).
4. (42:6).
5. (42:6).
6. (42:8).
7. (42:17).
8. (42:9).
9. (42:13).
10. (42:15).
11. (42:18,20).
12. (42:21).
13. (42:22).
14. (42:24).
15. (42:24).
16. (42:28).
17. (42:28).
18. (42:36).
19. (see Genesis 27).
20. (see 43:1-10).
21. (see 43:11-12).
22. (43:13-14).

CHAPTER **13: The Game Ends**
1. (Genesis 43:18).
2. (43:22).
3. (43:23).
4. (43:29).
5. (43:30).
6. (43:33-34).
7. (44:4).
8. (44:7-8).
9. (44:9).

10. (44:10).
11. (44:13).
12. (44:14).
13. (44:16, emphasis added).
14. (44:20).
15. (44:27-28).
16. (44:29).
17. (44:30).
18. (44:34).
19. (Genesis 45:1).
20. (45:2).
21. (45:5-7, emphasis added).
22. (45:8).
23. (Psalm 135:6).
24. (Isaiah 45:6-7).
25. (Psalm 66:10-12).
26. (1 Corinthians 4:5).
27. (2 Corinthians 5:10).

CHAPTER 14: Brokenness, Rescue, and Reunion
1. (Psalm 51:16-17).
2. (2 Corinthians 7:9-10).
3. Alan E. Nelson, *Embracing Brokenness* (Colorado Springs, CO: NavPress, 2002).
4. (Psalm 51:10-12).
5. (Genesis 45:9-11).
6. (45:14-15).
7. (45:18).
8. (45:23-24).
9. (45:26-28).
10. (Genesis 46:2-4).
11. (45:29).
12. (see Deuteronomy 8).
13. (John 8:11, NKJV).
14. (Numbers 32:23).

CHAPTER 15: **Honor and Rescue**
1. (Just as Joseph warned his brothers in Genesis 45:11).
2. (see Genesis 47:5-6).
3. (47:7,10).
4. (see 48:9,15).
5. (1 Timothy 2:2).
6. (Romans 13:4).
7. (Genesis 47:18).
8. (see 47:20-21).
9. (47:25).
10. (see 41:33-36).
11. (Ephesians 6:2).

CHAPTER 16: **Blessing**
1. (Genesis 47:27).
2. (47:28-30).
3. (47:31, MSG).
4. (Genesis 48:10).
5. (48:3-4, MSG).
6. (48:5-7, MSG).
7. (48:15-16).
8. (48:21).
9. (Genesis 49:22-26).
10. Gary Smalley and John Trent, *The Blessing* (Nashville, TN: Thomas Nelson, 1986), 9.
11. (1 Thessalonians 1:2).
12. (Colossians 1:9-11).
13. Jim Stovall, *The Ultimate Gift* (Colorado Springs, CO: David C. Cook, 2007).
14. James M. Barrie, famequote.com.
15. Alex Haley, *The Maroon*, quoted in *Reader's Digest*, December 1987, 45.
16. Philip Yancey, *What's So Amazing About Grace?* (Grand Rapids, MI: Zondervan, 1997), 38.

CHAPTER **17**: Acting with Grace

1. (Genesis 50:1).
2. (50:15).
3. (Acts 24:16).
4. (Hebrews 9:14).
5. (Genesis 50:16-17).
6. (50:17).
7. (50:18).
8. (50:19-20).
9. (Colossians 4:6).
10. (Ephesians 4:29).
11. (James 3:4-6, MSG).
12. (Romans 4:13-16, MSG).
13. (Ephesians 2:4-5,8).
14. (Luke 23:34).
15. (Colossians 3:13).
16. (Genesis 45:7; 50:20).

CHAPTER **18**: Faithful to the End

1. (Genesis 50:24).
2. (50:25).
3. (Exodus 13:19).
4. (Joshua 24:32).
5. (Hebrews 11:22).
6. (Exodus 1:8).
7. (Proverbs 13:12).
8. (Colossians 3:1).
9. (Psalm 39:7).
10. (Romans 5:1-5).
11. (see Hebrews 6:19–8:2).
12. (1 Peter 1:13)

AUTHOR

JERRY WHITE, international president emeritus of The Navigators, is a popular speaker at conferences and churches. He received a bachelor of science in electrical engineering from the University of Washington and a Ph.D. in astronautics from Purdue University. Dr. White served as a mission controller at Cape Canaveral, taught at the U.S. Air Force Academy, and retired from the Air Force in 1997 as a major general. He has authored several books, including *Making Peace with Reality* (2002).

More great titles from NavPress!

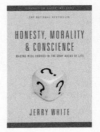

Honesty, Morality, and Conscience
Jerry White
978-1-60006-218-6

In *Honesty, Morality, and Conscience*, Jerry White takes a hard look at some of life's gray areas. Exploring the origin and depth of our conscience, our moral compass, and truthful living, he explains how God has given us everything we need to face the moral and ethical questions of today in all areas of our lives. Study guide included.

Souvenirs of Solitude
Brennan Manning
978-1-60006-867-6

The most reliable guides of spiritual formation pinpoint solitude and silence as central to the spiritual life. Now Brennan Manning—in his honest, original, and winning way—shares from his own experiences to prompt the reader into the riches of spending time alone with God.

Christian Coaching, Second Edition
[revised and updated]
Gary R. Collins, PhD
978-1-60006-361-9

Dr. Gary R. Collins takes the successful principles of coaching and gives them a God-centered application. Broader in scope than either mentoring or discipling, Christian coaching helps people find God's vision for their lives and learn to live accordingly.

To order copies, call NavPress at 1-800-366-7788
or log on to www.navpress.com.